the integral vision

the integral vision

A Very Short Introduction
to the Revolutionary Integral Approach
to Life, God, the Universe, and Everything

Ken Wilber

SHAMBHALA
Boston & London
2007

SHAMBHALA PUBLICATIONS, INC.
Horticultural Hall
300 Massachusetts Avenue
Boston, Massachusetts 02115
www.shambhala.com

Cover design by Paul Salamone.
See pages 231–32 for further illustration and design credits.

13 12 11 10 9 8 7 6 5

Printed in China

⊗ This edition is printed on acid-free paper that meets the
American National Standards Institute Z39.48 Standard.
♻ Shambhala makes every effort to print on recycled paper.
For more information please visit www.shambhala.com.
Distributed in the United States by Penguin Random House LLC
and in Canada by Random House of Canada Ltd

Library of Congress Cataloging-in-Publication Data
Wilber, Ken.
The integral vision: a very short introduction to the revolutionary
integral approach to life, God, the universe, and everything / Ken
Wilber.—1st ed.
    p.   cm.
ISBN 978-1-59030-475-4 (pbk.: alk. paper)
1. Spiritual life. I. Title.
BL624.W534 2007
191—dc22
                          2006051297

With special thanks to the staff of Integral Institute, whose tireless work, intelligence, passion, and creativity are helping make the Integral Vision a reality for all who wish to join in the AQAL adventure.

contents

chapter

1

INTRODUCTION

How can I navigate the 21st Century?

How can *WE* make *SENSE* of our own LIFE and AWARENESS?

What if I had a comprehensive map of myself and the brave new world I find myself in?

DURING THE LAST 30 YEARS, WE HAVE WITNESSED A HISTORICAL first: all of the world's cultures are now available to us. In the past, if you were born, say, a Chinese, you likely spent your entire life in one culture, often in one province, sometimes in one house, living and loving and dying on one small plot of land. But today, not only are people geographically mobile, but we can study, and have studied, virtually every known culture on the planet. In the global village, all cultures are exposed to each other.

Knowledge itself is now global. This means that, also for the first time, the sum total of human knowledge is available to us—the knowledge, experience, wisdom, and reflection of all major human civilizations—premodern, modern, and postmodern—are open to study by anyone.

What if we took literally everything that all the various cultures have to tell us about human potential—about spiritual growth, psychological growth, social growth—and put it all on the table? What if we attempted to find the critically essential keys to human growth, based on the sum total of human knowledge now open to us? What if we attempted, based on extensive cross-cultural study, to use all of the world's great traditions to create a composite map, a comprehensive map, an all-inclusive or *integral* map that included the best elements from all of them?

Sound complicated, complex, daunting? In a sense, it is. But in another sense, the results turn out to be surprisingly simple and elegant. Over the last several decades, there has indeed been an extensive search for a comprehensive map of human potentials. This map uses all the known systems and models of human growth—from the ancient shamans and sages to today's breakthroughs in cognitive science— and distills their major components into 5 simple factors, factors that are the essential elements or keys to unlocking and facilitating human evolution.

Welcome to the Integral Approach.

An Integral or Comprehensive Map

What are these 5 elements? We call them **quadrants**, **levels**, **lines**, **states**, and **types**. As you will see, all of these elements are, right now, *available in your own awareness*. These 5 elements are not merely theoretical concepts; they are aspects of your own experience, contours of your own consciousness, as you can easily verify for yourself as we proceed.

What is the point of using this Integral Map? First, whether you are working in business, medicine, psychotherapy, law, ecology, or simply everyday living and learning, the Integral Map helps make sure that you are "touching all the bases." If you are trying to fly over the Rocky Mountains, the more accurate a map you have, the less likely you will crash. An Integral

Approach ensures that you are utilizing the full range of resources for any situation, with the greater likelihood of success.

Second, if you learn to spot these 5 elements in your own awareness—and because they are there in any event—then you can more easily appreciate them, exercise them, use them . . . and thereby vastly accelerate your own growth and development to higher, wider, deeper ways of being, not to mention greater excellence and achievement in work and professional life. A simple familiarity with the 5 elements in the Integral Model will help you orient yourself more easily and fully in this exciting journey of discovery and awakening.

In short, the Integral Approach helps you see both yourself and the world around you in more comprehensive and effective ways. But one thing is important to realize from the start. The Integral Map is just a map. It is not the territory. We certainly don't want to confuse the map with the territory—but neither do we want to be working with an inaccurate or faulty map. Do you want to fly over the Rockies with a bad map? The Integral Map is just a map, but it is the most complete and accurate map we have at this time.

What Is an IOS?

IOS simply means **Integral Operating System**. In an information network, an operating system is the infrastructure that allows various software programs to operate. We use **Integral Operating System** or **IOS** as another phrase for the Integral Map. The point is simply that, if you are running any "software" in your life—such as your business, work, play, or relationships—you want the best operating system you can find, and **IOS** fits that bill. In touching all the bases, it allows the most effective programs to be used. This is just another way of talking about the comprehensive and inclusive nature of the Integral Model.

We will also be exploring what is perhaps the most important use of the Integral Map or Operating System. Because an IOS can be used to help index any activity —from art to dance to business to psychology to politics to ecology to spirituality—it allows each of those domains to talk to the others. Using IOS, business has the terminology with which to communicate fully with ecology, which can communicate with art, which can communicate with law, which can communicate with poetry and education and medicine and spirituality. In the history of humankind, this has never really happened before.

By using the Integral Approach—by using an Integral Map or Integral Operating System—we are able to facilitate and dramatically accelerate cross-disciplinary and trans-disciplinary knowledge, thus creating the world's first truly integral learning community: Integral Institute. And when it comes to religion and spirituality, using the Integral Approach has allowed the creation of Integral Spiritual Center, where some of the world's leading spiritual teachers from all major religions have come together not only to listen to each other but to "teach the teachers," resulting in one of the most extraordinary learning events imaginable. We will return to this important gathering, and ways you can join in this community if you wish.

But it all starts with these simple 5 elements in the contours of your own consciousness.

chapter

2

THE MAIN INGREDIENTS

What are the
essential
ASPECTS
of my own
awareness,

right now?

INGREDIENTS

TOUR

In the Introduction, we said that all of the 5 elements of the Integral Map are available, right now, in your own awareness. What follows is therefore, in a sense, a guided tour of your own experience. So why don't you come along and see if you can spot some of these features arising in your own awareness right now.

SOME OF THE FEATURES OF THE INTEGRAL MAP REFFR TO subjective realities in you, some refer to objective realities out there in the world, and others refer to collective or communal realities shared with others. Let's start with states of consciousness, which refer to subjective realities.

States of Consciousness

Everybody is familiar with major **states of consciousness**, such as waking, dreaming, and deep sleep. Right now, you are in a waking state of consciousness (or, if you are tired, perhaps a daydream state of consciousness). There are all sorts of different states of consciousness, including *meditative states* (induced by yoga, contemplative prayer, meditation, and so on), *altered states* (such as drug-induced), and a variety of *peak experiences*, many of which can be triggered by intense experiences like making love, walking in nature, or listening to exquisite music.

The great wisdom traditions (such as Christian mysticism, Vedanta Hinduism, Vajrayana Buddhism, and Jewish Kabbalah) maintain that the 3 *natural states* of consciousness—waking, dreaming, and deep formless sleep—actually contain a treasure trove of spiritual wisdom and spiritual awakening . . . if we know how to use them correctly. We usually think of the

peak experiences:
lightning strikes!

dream state as less real, but what if you could enter it while awake? And the same with deep sleep? Might you learn something extraordinary in those awakened states? In a special sense, which we will explore as we go along, the 3 great natural states of waking, dreaming, and deep sleep might contain an entire spectrum of spiritual enlightenment. You've probably heard of satori, yes?, which is a Zen term for a profound experience of spiritual awakening, which is said to contain the ultimate secrets—or secret—of the universe itself.

But on a much simpler, more mundane level, everybody experiences various states of consciousness, and these states often provide profound motivation, meaning, and drives, in both yourself and others. Think of the many "aha!" experiences of brilliantly creative insight: what if we could tap into those whenever needed for intense problem solving? In any particular situation, states of consciousness may not be a very important factor, or they may be the determining factor, but no integral approach can afford to ignore them. Whenever you are using **IOS**, you will automatically be prompted to check and see if you are touching bases with these important subjective realities. This is an example of how a map—in this case, the IOS or Integral Map—can help you look for territory you might not have even suspected was there, and then give you tools to navigate it. . . .

Stages or Levels of Development

There's an interesting thing about states of consciousness: they come and they go. Even great peak experiences or altered states, no matter how profound, will come, stay a bit, then pass. No matter how wonderful their capacities, they are temporary.

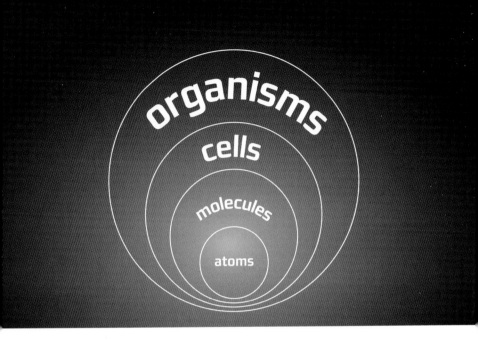

Figure 1. *Levels: All Development Is Envelopment.*

Where states of consciousness are temporary, **stages of consciousness** are permanent. Stages represent the actual milestones of growth and development. Once you are at a stage, it is an enduring acquisition. For example, once a child develops through the linguistic stages of development, the child has permanent access to language. Language isn't a peak experience, present one minute and gone the next. The same thing happens with other types of growth. Once you stably reach a stage of growth and development, you can access the capacities of that stage—such as greater consciousness, more embracing love, higher ethical callings, greater intelligence and awareness—virtually any time you want. *Passing states* have become *permanent traits*.

How many stages of development are there? Well, remember that in any map, the way you divide and represent the actual territory is somewhat arbitrary. For example, how many degrees are there between freezing and boiling water? If you use a Centigrade scale or "map," there are 100 degrees between freezing and boiling. But if you use a Fahrenheit scale, freezing is at 32 and boiling is at 212, so there are 180 degrees between them. Which is right? Both of them. It just depends upon how you want to slice that pie.

The same is true of stages. There are all sorts of ways to slice and dice development, and therefore there are all sorts of **stage conceptions**. All of them can be useful. In the chakra system of Yoga philosophy, for example, there are 7 major stages or levels of consciousness. Jean Gebser, a famous anthropologist, gave 5: archaic, magic, mythic, rational, and integral. Certain Western psychological models have 8, 12, or more levels of development. Which is right? All of them; it just depends on what you want to keep track of in growth and development.

"**Stages** of development" are also referred to as "**levels** of development," the idea being that each stage represents a level of organization or a level of complexity. For example, in the sequence from atoms to molecules to cells to organisms, each of those stages of evolution involves a greater level of complexity. The word "level" is not meant in a judgmental or exclusionary fashion, but simply to indicate that there are important *emergent* qualities that tend to come into being in a discrete or quantum-like fashion, and these developmental jumps or levels are important aspects of many natural phenomena.

And, most importantly, to emphasize the fluid and flowing nature of stages, we often refer to them as **waves**. Stages or waves of development are an important ingredient of IOS. Generally, in the Integral Model, we work with around 8 to 10 levels, stages, or waves of consciousness development. We have found, after years of field work, that more stages than that are too cumbersome, and less than that, too vague. Some of the stage conceptions we often use include those of self development pioneered by Jane Loevinger and Susanne Cook-Greuter; Spiral Dynamics, by Don Beck and Christopher Cowan; and orders of consciousness, researched by Robert Kegan. But there are many other useful stage conceptions available with the Integral Approach, and you can adopt any of them that are appropriate to your situation.

As we get into the specifics later in this book, you will see how incredibly important stages can be. But let's take a simple example now to show what is involved.

Egocentric, Ethnocentric, and Worldcentric

To grasp what is involved with levels or stages, let's use a very simple model possessing only 3 of them. If we look at moral development, for example, we find that an infant at birth has not yet been socialized into the culture's ethics and conventions; this is called the **preconventional stage**. It is also called **egocentric**, in that the infant's awareness is largely self-absorbed. But as the young child begins to learn its culture's rules and norms, it grows into the **conventional stage** of morals. This stage is also called **ethnocentric**, in that it centers on the child's particular group, tribe, clan, or nation, and it therefore tends to exclude those not of its group. But at the next major stage of moral development, the **postconventional stage**, the individual's identity expands once again, this time to include a care and concern for all peoples, regardless of race, color, sex, or creed, which is why this stage is also called **worldcentric**.

Thus, moral development tends to move from "me" (egocentric) to "us" (ethnocentric) to "all of us" (worldcentric)—a good example of the unfolding waves of consciousness.

Another way to picture these 3 stages is as **body**, **mind**, and **spirit**. Those words all have many different and valid

WORLDCENTRIC

ETHNOCENTRIC

EGOCENTRIC

"Me"

"Us"

"All of Us"

Figure 2. *Psychological Development Also Is Envelopment.*

meanings, but when used specifically to refer to stages, they mean:

Stage 1, which is dominated by my gross physical reality, is the "body" stage (using body in its typical meaning of physical body). Since you are identified merely with the separate bodily organism and its survival drives, this is also the "me" or egocentric stage.

Stage 2 is the "mind" stage, where identity expands from the isolated gross body and starts to share relationships with many others, based perhaps on shared values, mutual interests, common ideals, or shared dreams. Because I can use the mind to take the role of others—to put myself in their shoes and feel what it is like to be them—my identity expands from "me" to "us" (the move from egocentric to ethnocentric).

With stage 3, my identity expands once again, this time from an identity with "us" to an identity with "all of us" (the move from ethnocentric to worldcentric). Here I begin to understand that, in addition to the wonderful diversity of humans and cultures, there are also similarities and shared commonalities. Discovering the commonwealth of all beings is the move from ethnocentric to worldcentric, and is "spiritual" in the sense of things common to all sentient beings.

That is one way to view the unfolding from body to mind to spirit, where each of them is considered as a stage, wave, or level of unfolding care and consciousness, moving from egocentric to ethnocentric to worldcentric.

We will be returning to stages of evolution and development, each time exploring them from a new angle. For now, all that is required is to understand that by "stages" we mean progressive and permanent milestones along the evolutionary path of your own unfolding. Whether we talk stages of consciousness, stages of energy, stages of culture, stages of spiritual realization, stages of moral development, and so on, we are talking of these important and fundamental rungs in the unfolding of your higher, deeper, wider potentials.

Whenever you use IOS, you will automatically be prompted to check and see if you have included the important **stage aspects** of any situation, which will dramatically increase your likelihood of success, whether that success be measured in terms of personal transformation, social change, excellence in business, care for others, or simple satisfaction in life.

Lines of Development: I'm Good at Some Things, Not-So-Good at Others . . .

Have you ever noticed how unevenly developed virtually all of us are? Some people are highly developed in, say, logical thinking, but poorly developed in emotional feelings. Some people have highly advanced cognitive development (they're very smart) but poor moral development (they're mean and ruthless). Some people excel in emotional intelligence, but can't add 2 plus 2.

Howard Gardner made this concept fairly well known using the idea of **multiple intelligences**. Human beings have a variety of intelligences, such as cognitive intelligence, emotional intelligence, musical intelligence, kinesthetic intelligence, and so on. Most people excel in one or two of those, but do poorly in the others. This is not necessarily or even usually a bad thing; part of integral wisdom is finding where we excel and thus where we can best offer the world our deepest gifts.

But this does mean that we need to be aware of our strengths (or the intelligences with which we can shine) as well as our weaknesses (where we do poorly or even pathologically). And this brings us to another of our 5 essential elements: our multiple intelligences or developmental lines. So far we have looked at **states** and **stages**; what are **lines** or multiple intelligences?

Various multiple intelligences include: cognitive, interpersonal, moral, emotional, and aesthetic. Why are these also called **developmental lines**? Because those intelligences show growth and development. They unfold in progressive stages. What are those progressive stages? The stages we just outlined.

In other words, each multiple intelligence grows—or can grow—through the 3 major stages (or through any of the stages of any of the developmental models, whether 3 stages, 5 stages, 7 or more; remember, these are all like Centigrade and Fahrenheit). You can have cognitive development to stage 1, to stage 2, and to stage 3, for example.

Likewise with the other intelligences. Emotional development to stage 1 means that you have developed the capacity for emotions centering on "me," especially the emotions and drives of hunger, survival, and self-protection. If you continue to grow emotionally from stage 1 to stage 2— or from egocentric to ethnocentric—you will expand from "me" to "us," and begin to develop emotional commitments and attachments to loved ones, members of your family, close friends, perhaps your whole tribe or whole nation. If you grow into stage-3 emotions, you will develop the further capacity for a care and compassion that reaches beyond your own tribe or nation and attempts to include all human beings and even all sentient beings in a worldcentric care and compassion.

And remember, because these are stages, you have attained them in a permanent fashion. Before that happens, any of these capacities will be merely passing states: you will plug into some of them, if at all, in a temporary fashion— great peak experiences of expanded knowing and being, wondrous "aha!" experiences, profound altered glimpses into your own higher possibilities. But with practice, you will convert those states into stages, or permanent traits in the territory of you.

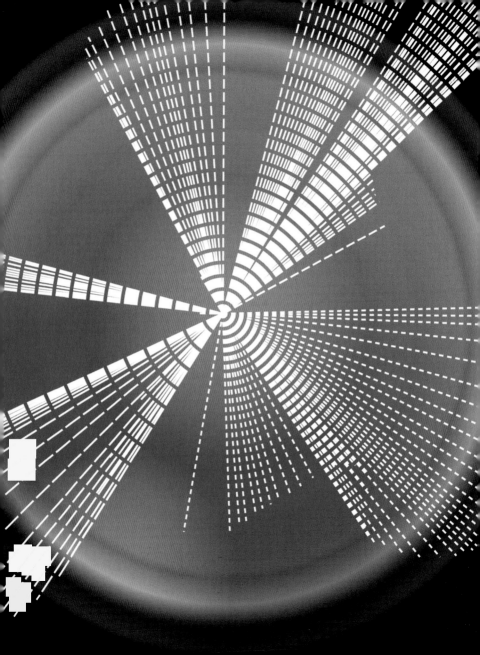

The Integral Psychograph

There is a fairly easy way to represent these intelligences or multiple lines. In figure 3 (p. 42), we have drawn a simple graph showing the 3 major stages (or **levels** of development) and 5 of the most important intelligences (or **lines** of development). **Through the major stages or levels of development, the various lines unfold.** The 3 levels or stages can apply to any developmental line—sexual, cognitive, spiritual, emotional, moral, and so on. The level of a particular line simply means the "altitude" of that line in terms of its growth and consciousness. This is why people often say, "That person is highly developed morally," or "That person is really advanced spiritually."

In figure 3, we have shown somebody who excels in cognitive development and is good at interpersonal development, but does poorly in moral and really poorly in emotional intelligence. Other individuals would, of course, have a different "psychograph."

The **psychograph** helps to spot where your greatest potentials are. You very likely already know what you excel in and what you don't. But part of the Integral Approach is learning to refine considerably this knowledge of your own contours, so that you can more confidently deal with your own strengths and weaknesses as well as those of others.

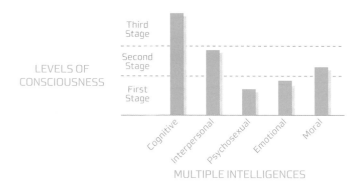

Figure 3. *A Psychograph.*

The psychograph also helps us spot the ways that virtually all of us are unevenly developed, and this helps prevent us from thinking that just because we are terrific in one area we must be terrific in all the others. In fact, usually the opposite. More than one leader, spiritual teacher, or politician has spectacularly crashed through lack of an understanding of these simple realities.

To be "integrally developed" does not mean that you have to excel in all the known intelligences, or that all of your lines have to be at level 3. But it does mean that you develop a very good sense of what your own psychograph is actually like, so that with a much more integral self-image you can plan your future development. For some people, this will indeed mean strengthening certain intelligences that are so weak they are causing problems. For others, it will mean clearing up a serious problem or pathology in one line (such as the psychosexual). And for others, simply recognizing where their strengths and weaknesses lie, and planning accordingly. Using an integral map, we can scope out our own psychographs with more assurance.

Thus, to be **"integrally informed"** does not mean you have to master all lines of development, just be aware of them. If you then choose to remedy any unbalances, that is part of Integral Life Practice (ILP), which actually helps to increase levels of consciousness and development using a remarkably effective "spiritual cross-training" approach. (We will be discussing ILP in detail in chap. 6.)

Notice another very important point. In certain types of psychological and spiritual training, you can be introduced to a full spectrum of **states** of consciousness and bodily experiences right from the start—as a peak experience, meditative state, shamanic vision, altered state, and so on. The reason these peak experiences are possible is that many of the major states of consciousness (such as waking-gross, dreaming-subtle, and formless-causal) are ever-present possibilities. So you can very quickly be introduced to many **higher states** of consciousness.

You cannot, however, be introduced to all the qualities of **higher stages** without actual growth and practice. You can have a peak experience of higher *states* (like seeing an interior subtle light or having a feeling of oneness with all of nature), because many states are ever-present, and so they can be "peek"-experienced right now. But you cannot have a peak experience of a higher *stage* (like being a concert-level pianist), because stages unfold sequentially and take considerable time to develop. Stages build upon their predecessors in very concrete ways, so they cannot be skipped: like atoms to molecules to cells to organisms, you can't go from atoms to cells and skip molecules. This is one of the many important differences between states and stages.

However, with repeated practice of contacting higher states, your own stages of development will tend to unfold in a much faster and easier way. There is, in fact, considerable experimental evidence demonstrating exactly that. The more you are plunged into authentic higher *states* of consciousness—such as meditative states—the *faster* you will grow and develop through any of the *stages* of consciousness. It is as if higher-states training acts as a lubricant on the spiral of development, helping you to disidentify with a lower stage so that the next higher stage can emerge, until you can stably remain at higher levels of awareness on an ongoing basis, whereupon a passing state has become a permanent trait. These types of higher-states training, such as meditation, are a part of any integral approach to transformation.

In short, you cannot skip actual *stages*, but you can accelerate your growth through them by using various types of *state*-practices, such as meditation, and these transformative practices are an important part of the Integral Approach.

What Type: Boy or Girl?

The next component of the "Comprehensive Map of the Territory of You" is easy: each of the previous components has a masculine and feminine type.

Types simply refers to items that can be present at virtually any stage or state. One common typology, for example, is the Myers-Briggs (whose main types are feeling, thinking, sensing, and intuiting). **You can be any of those types at virtually any stage of development.** These kind of "horizontal typologies" can be very useful, especially when combined with levels, lines, and states. To show what is involved, we can use "masculine" and "feminine" as one example of types.

Carol Gilligan, in her enormously influential book *In a Different Voice*, pointed out that both men and women tend to develop through 3 or 4 major levels or stages of moral development. Pointing to a great deal of research evidence, Gilligan noted that these 3 or 4 moral stages can be called *preconventional*, *conventional*, *postconventional*, and *integrated*. These are actually quite similar to the 3 simple developmental stages we are using, this time applied to moral intelligence.

Gilligan found that stage 1 is a morality centered entirely on "me" (hence this preconventional stage or level is also called **egocentric**). Stage-2 moral development is centered on "us," so that my identity has expanded from just me to include other human beings of my group (hence this conventional stage is often called **ethnocentric**, traditional, or conformist). With stage-3 moral development, my identity expands once again, this time from "us" to "all of us," or all human beings (or even all sentient beings)—and hence this stage is often called **worldcentric**. I now have care and compassion, not just for me (egocentric), and not just for my family, my tribe, or my nation (ethnocentric), but for all of humanity, for all men and women everywhere, regardless of race, color, sex, or creed (worldcentric). And if I develop even further, at stage-4 moral development, which Gilligan calls **integrated**, then . . .

Well, before we look at the important conclusion of Gilligan's work, let's first note her major contribution. Gilligan strongly agreed that women, like men, develop through those 3 or 4 major hierarchical stages of growth. Gilligan herself correctly refers to these stages as *hierarchical* because each stage has a *higher* capacity for care and compassion. But she said that women progress through those stages using a different type of logic—they develop "in a different voice."

Male logic, or a man's voice, tends to be based on terms of autonomy, justice, and rights; whereas women's logic or voice tends to be based on terms of relationship, care, and responsibility. Men tend toward agency; women tend toward communion. Men follow rules; women follow connections. Men look; women touch. Men tend toward individualism, women toward relationship. One of Gilligan's favorite stories: A little boy and girl are playing. The boy says, "Let's play pirates!" The girl says, "Let's play like we live next door to each other." Boy: "No, I want to play pirates!" "Okay, you play the pirate who lives next door."

Little boys don't like girls around when they are playing games like baseball, because the two voices clash badly, and often hilariously. Some boys are playing baseball, a kid takes his third strike and is out, so he starts to cry. The other boys stand unmoved until the kid stops crying; after all, a rule is a rule, and the rule is: three strikes and you're out. Gilligan points out that if a girl is around, she will usually say, "Ah, come on, give him another try!" The girl sees him crying and wants to help, wants to connect, wants to heal. This, however, drives the boys nuts, who are doing this game as an initiation into the world of rules and male logic. Gilligan says that the boys will hurt feelings in order to save the rules; the girls will break the rules in order to save the feelings.

In a different voice. Both the girls and boys will develop through the 3 or 4 developmental stages of moral growth (egocentric to ethnocentric to worldcentric to integrated), but they will do so in a different voice, using a different logic. Gilligan specifically calls these hierarchical stages in women **selfish** (which is egocentric), **care** (which is ethnocentric), **universal care** (which is worldcentric), and **integrated**. Again, why did Gilligan (who has been badly misunderstood on this topic) say that these stages are hierarchical? Because each stage has a higher capacity for care and compassion. (Not all hierarchies are bad, and this is a good example of why.)

So, integrated or stage 4—what is that? At the 4th and highest wave of moral development, according to Gilligan, the masculine and feminine voices in each of us tend to become integrated. This does not mean that a person at this stage starts to lose the distinctions between masculine and feminine, and hence become a kind of bland, androgynous, asexual being. In fact, masculine and feminine dimensions might become more intensified. But it does mean the individuals start to befriend both the masculine and feminine modes in themselves, even if they characteristically act predominantly from one or the other.

Have you ever seen a *caduceus* (the symbol of the medical profession)? It's a staff with two serpents crisscrossing it, and wings at the top of the staff (see p. 49). The staff itself represents the central spinal column; where the serpents cross the staff represents the individual chakras moving up

Caduceus.

the spine from the lowest to the highest; and the two serpents themselves represent solar and lunar (or masculine and feminine) energies *at each of the chakras.*

That's the crucial point. The 7 chakras, which are simply a more complex version of the 3 simple levels or stages, represent 7 levels of consciousness and energy available to all human beings. (The first three chakras—food, sex, and power—are roughly stage 1; chakras 4 and 5—relational heart and communication—are basically stage 2; and chakras 6 and 7—psychic and spiritual—are the epitome of stage 3). The important point here is that, according to the traditions, **each of those 7 levels has a masculine and feminine mode** (aspect, type, or "voice"). Neither masculine nor feminine is higher or better; they are two equivalent types at each of the levels of consciousness.

This means, for example, that with chakra 3 (the egocentric power chakra), there is a masculine and feminine version of the same chakra: at that chakra-level, males tend toward power exercised autonomously ("My way or the highway!"), women tend toward power exercised communally or socially ("Do it this way or I won't talk to you"). And so on with the other major chakras, each of them having a solar and lunar, or masculine and feminine, dimension. Neither is more fundamental; neither can be ignored.

At the 7th chakra, however, notice that the masculine and feminine serpents both disappear into their ground or source. Masculine and feminine meet and unite at the crown—they literally become one. And that is what Gilligan found with her stage-4 moral development: the two voices in each person become integrated, so that there is a paradoxical union of autonomy and relationship, rights and responsibilities, agency and communion, wisdom and compassion, justice and mercy, masculine and feminine.

The important point is that whenever you use IOS, you are automatically checking any situation—in yourself, in others, in an organization, in a culture—and making sure that you include both the masculine and feminine types so as to be as comprehensive and inclusive as possible. If you believe that there are no major differences between masculine and feminine—or if you are suspicious of such differences—then that is fine, too, and you can treat them the same if you want. We are simply saying that, in either case, make sure you touch bases with both the masculine and feminine, however you view them.

But more than that, there are numerous other "horizontal typologies" that can be very helpful when part of a comprehensive IOS (Myers-Briggs, enneagram, etc.), and the Integral Approach draws on any or all of those typologies as appropriate. "Types" are as important as quadrants, levels, lines, and states.

Sick Boy, Sick Girl

There's an interesting thing about types. You can have healthy and unhealthy versions of them. To say that somebody is caught in an unhealthy type is not a way to judge them but a way to understand and communicate more clearly and effectively with them.

For example, if each stage of development has a masculine and feminine dimension, each of those can be healthy or unhealthy, which we sometimes call "sick boy, sick girl." This is simply another kind of horizontal typing, but one that can be extremely useful.

If the healthy masculine principle tends toward autonomy, strength, independence, and freedom, when that principle becomes unhealthy or pathological, all of those positive

"Katia, I know that with the right combination of therapy and medication I could have a committed relationship with you."

virtues either over- or underfire. There is not just autonomy, but alienation; not just strength, but domination; not just independence, but morbid fear of relationship and commitment; not just a drive toward freedom, but a drive to destroy. The unhealthy masculine principle does not transcend in freedom, but dominates in fear.

If the healthy feminine principle tends toward flowing,

relationship, care, and compassion, the unhealthy feminine flounders in each of those. Instead of being in relationship, she becomes lost in relationship. Instead of a healthy self in communion with others, she loses her self altogether and is dominated by the relationships she is in. Not a connection, but a fusion; not a flow state, but a panic state; not a communion, but a meltdown. The unhealthy feminine principle does not find fullness in connection, but chaos in fusion.

Using IOS, you will find ways to identify both the healthy and unhealthy masculine and feminine dimensions operating in yourself and in others. But the important point about this section is simple: various typologies have their usefulness in helping us to understand and communicate with others. And with any typology, there are healthy and unhealthy versions of a type. Pointing to an unhealthy type is not a way to judge people, but a way to understand and communicate with them more clearly and effectively.

There's Even Room for Many Bodies

Let's return now to states of consciousness in order to make a final point before bringing this all together in an integral conclusion.

States of consciousness do not hover in the air, dangling and disembodied. On the contrary, every mind has its body. For every state of consciousness, there is a felt energetic component, an embodied feeling, a concrete vehicle that provides the actual support for any state of awareness.

Let's use a simple example from the wisdom traditions. Because each of us has the 3 great states of consciousness— waking, dreaming, and formless sleep—the wisdom traditions maintain that each of us likewise has **3 bodies**, which are often called the **gross body**, the **subtle body**, and the **causal body**.

I have 3 bodies? Are you kidding me? Isn't one body enough? But keep in mind a few things. For the wisdom tra-

ditions, a "body" simply means a mode of experience or energetic feeling. So there is coarse or gross experience, subtle or refined experience, and very subtle or causal experience. These are what philosophers would call "phenomenological realities," or realities as they present themselves to our immediate awareness. Right now, you have access to a gross body and its gross energy, a subtle body and its subtle energy, and a causal body and its causal energy.

What's an example of these 3 bodies? Notice that, right now, you are in a *waking state* of awareness; as such, you are aware of your **gross body**—the physical, material, sensorimotor body. But when you dream at night, there is no gross physical body; it seems to have vanished. You are aware in the dream state, yet you don't have a gross body of dense matter but a **subtle body** of light, energy, emotional feelings, fluid and flowing images. In the dream state, the mind and soul are set free to create as they please, to imagine vast worlds not tied to gross sensory realities but reaching out, almost magically, to touch other souls, other people and far-off places, wild and radiant images cascading to the rhythm of the heart's desire. So what kind of body do you have in the dream? Well, a **subtle body** of feelings, images, even light. That's what you feel like in the dream. And dreams are not "just illusion." When somebody like Martin Luther King, Jr., says, "I have a dream," that is a good example of tapping into the great potential of visionary dreaming, where the subtle body and mind are set free to soar to their highest possibilities.

As you pass from the *dream state* with its subtle body into the deep-sleep or *formless state*, even thoughts and images drop away, and there is only a vast emptiness, a formless expanse beyond any individual "I" or ego or self. The great wisdom traditions maintain that in this state—which might seem like merely a blank or nothingness—we are actually plunged into a vast formless realm, a great Emptiness or Ground of Being, an expanse of consciousness that seems almost infinite. Along with this almost infinite expanse of consciousness there is an almost infinite body or energy—the **causal body**, the body of the finest, most subtle experience possible, a great formlessness out of which creative possibilities can arise.

Of course, many people do not experience that deep state in such a full fashion. But again, the traditions are unanimous that this *formless state* and its *causal body* can be entered in full awareness, whereupon they, too, yield their extraordinary potentials for growth and awareness.

The point, once again, is simply that whenever IOS is being utilized, it reminds us to check in with our waking-state realities, our subtle-state dreams and visions and innovative ideas, as well as our own open, formless ground of possibilities that is the source of so much creativity. The important point about the Integral Approach is that we want to touch bases with as many potentials as possible so as to miss nothing in terms of possible solutions, growth, and transformation.

Consciousness and Complexity

Perhaps 3 bodies are just too "far out"? Well, remember that these are phenomenological realities, or experiential realities, but there is a simpler, less far-out way to look at them, this time grounded in hard-headed science. It is this: *every level of interior consciousness is accompanied by a level of exterior physical complexity*. The greater the consciousness, the more complex the system housing it.

For example, in living organisms, the **reptilian brain stem** is accompanied by a rudimentary interior consciousness of basic drives such as food and hunger, physiological sensations, and sensorimotor actions (everything that we earlier called "gross," centered on the "me"). By the time we get to the more complex **mammalian limbic system**, basic sensations have expanded and evolved to include quite sophisticated feelings, desires, emotional-sexual impulses, and needs (hence the beginning of what we called subtle experience or the subtle body, which can expand from "me" to "us"). As evolution proceeds to even more complex physical structures, such as the **triune brain** with its **neocortex**, consciousness once again expands to a worldcentric awareness of "all of us" (and thus even begins to tap into what we called the causal body).

That is a very simple example of the fact that increasing interior consciousness is accompanied by increasing exterior

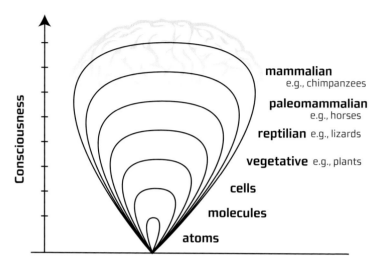

Figure 4. *Increasing Complexity Means Increasing Consciousness.*

complexity of the systems housing it. When using **IOS**, we often look at both the **interior levels of consciousness** and the corresponding **exterior levels of physical complexity**, since including both of them results in a much more balanced and inclusive approach.

We will see exactly what this means in the next chapter.

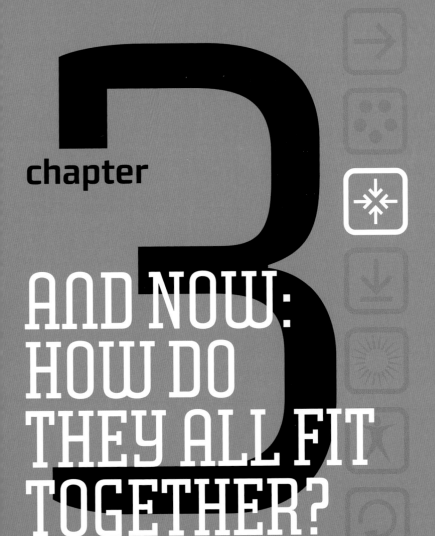

chapter

3

AND NOW: HOW DO THEY ALL FIT TOGETHER?

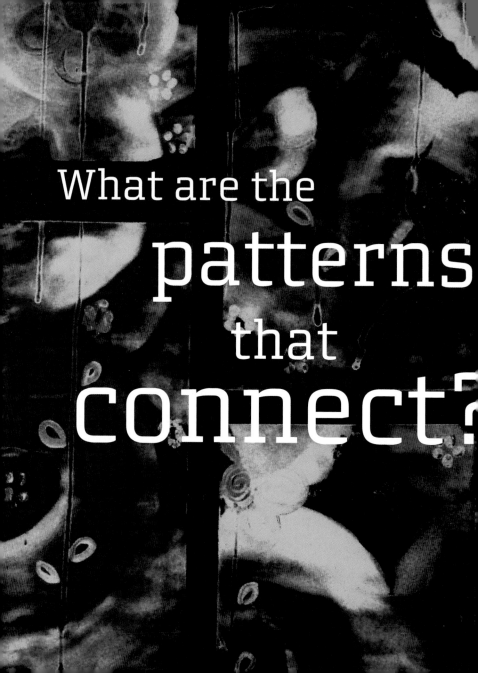

What are the
patterns
that
connect?

Let's start with...

...the four profound DIMENSIONS or PERSPECTIVES that hold your universe TOGETHER

IOS—and the Integral Model—would be not a "whole" but a "heap" if it did not suggest a way that all of these various components are related. How do they all fit together? It's one thing to simply lay all the pieces of the cross-cultural survey on the table and say, "They're all important!," and quite another to spot the patterns that actually connect all the pieces. Discovering the profound *patterns that connect* is a major accomplishment of the Integral Approach.

IN THIS SECTION, WE WILL BRIEFLY OUTLINE THESE PATTERNS, ALL of which together are sometimes referred to as **A-Q-A-L** (pronounced *ah-qwul*), which is shorthand for "all quadrants, all levels, all lines, all states, all types"—and those are simply the components that we have already outlined (except the quadrants, which we will get to momentarily). **AQAL** is just another term for **IOS** or the Integral Map, but one that is often used to specifically designate this particular approach.

At the beginning of this introduction, we said that all 5 components of the Integral Model were items that are *available to your awareness right now*, and this is true of the quadrants as well.

Did you ever notice that major languages have what are called 1st-person, 2nd-person, and 3rd-person pronouns? The **1st-person** perspective refers to "the person who is speaking," which includes pronouns like *I, me, mine* (in the singular) and *we, us, ours* (in the plural). The **2nd-person** perspective refers to "the person who is spoken to," which includes pronouns like *you* and *yours*. The **3rd-person** perspective refers to "the person or thing being spoken about," such as *he, him, she, her, they, them, it*, and *its*.

Thus, if I am speaking to you about my new car, "I" am 1st person, "you" are 2nd person, and the new car (or "it") is 3rd person. Now, if you and I are talking and communicating, we will indicate this by using, for example, the word "we," as in, "We understand each other." "We" is technically 1st-person plural, but if you and I are communicating, then your 2nd person and my 1st person are part of this extraordinary "we." Thus, 2nd person is sometimes indicated as "you/we," or "thou/we," or sometimes just "we."

So we can therefore simplify 1st-, 2nd-, and 3rd-person as **"I," "we,"** and **"it."**

That all seems trivial, doesn't it? Boring, maybe? So let's try this. Instead of saying "I," "we," and "it," what if we said the **Beautiful**, the **Good**, and the **True**? And what if we said that the Beautiful, the Good, and the True are dimensions of your very own being at each and every moment, including each and every level of growth and development? And that through an integral practice, you can discover deeper and deeper dimensions of your own Goodness, your own Truth, and your own Beauty?

Hmm, definitely more interesting. The Beautiful, the Good, and the True are simply variations on 1st-, 2nd-, and 3rd-person pronouns found in all major languages, and they are found in all major languages because Beauty, Truth, and Goodness are very real dimensions of reality to which language has adapted. The 3rd person (or "it") refers to objective Truth, which is best investigated by science. The 2nd person (or "you/we") refers to Goodness, or the ways that we—that you and I—treat each other, and whether we do so with decency, honesty, and respect. In other words, basic morality. And 1st person deals with the "I," with self and self-expression, art and aesthetics, and the Beauty that is in the eye (or the "I") of the beholder.

So the "I," "we," and "it" dimensions of experience really refer to **art**, **morals**, and **science**. Or **self**, **culture**, and **nature**. Or the **Beautiful**, the **Good**, and the **True**. (For some reason, philosophers always refer to those in this order: the Good, the True, and the Beautiful. Which order do you prefer? Any order is fine.)

The point is that *every* event in the manifest world *has all 3 of those dimensions*. You can look at any event from the point of view of the "I" (or how I personally see and feel about the event); from the point of view of the "we" (how not just I but others see the event); and as an "it" (or the objective facts of the event). Thus, an integrally informed path will take all of those dimensions into account, and thus arrive at a more comprehensive and effective approach—in the "I" and the "we" and the "it"—or in self and culture and nature.

If you leave out science, or leave out art, or leave out morals, something is going to be missing, something will get broken. Self and culture and nature are liberated together or not at all. So fundamental are these dimensions of "I," "we," and "it" that we call them the 4 quadrants, and we make them a foundation of the integral framework or IOS. (We arrive at "4" quadrants by subdividing "it" into singular "it" and plural "its.") A few diagrams will help clarify the basic points.

Figure 5 is a schematic of the 4 quadrants. It shows the **"I"** (the *inside* of the *individual*), the **"it"** (the *outside* of the *individual*), the **"we"** (the *inside* of the *collective*), and the **"its"** (the *outside* of the *collective*). In other words, the

Goodness

TRUTH

beauty

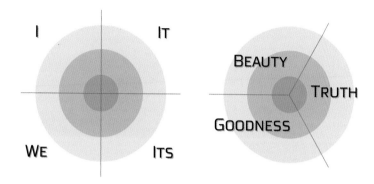

Figure 5. *The Quadrants.*

4 quadrants—which are the 4 fundamental perspectives on any occasion (or the 4 basic ways of looking at anything)—turn out to be fairly simple: they are the **inside** and the **outside** of the **individual** and the **collective**.

Figures 6 and 7 show a few of the details of the 4 quadrants. (Some of these are technical terms that needn't be bothered with for this basic introduction; simply peruse the diagrams and get a sense of the different types of items you might find in each of the quadrants.)

For example, in the **Upper-Left quadrant** (the interior of the individual), you find your own immediate thoughts, feelings, sensations, and so on (all described in 1st-person terms). But if you look at your individual being *from the outside*, in the terms not of subjective awareness but objective science, you find neurotransmitters, a limbic system, the neocortex, com-

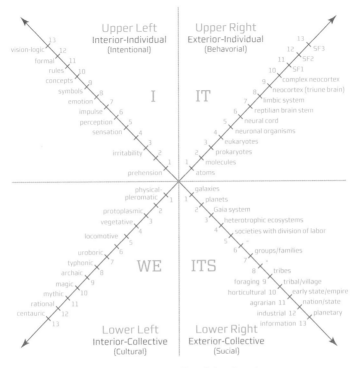

Figure 6. *Some Details of the Quadrants.*

plex molecular structures, cells, organ systems, DNA, and so on—all described in 3rd-person objective terms ("it" and "its"). The **Upper-Right quadrant** is therefore what any *individual* event looks like *from the outside*. This especially includes its physical behavior; its material components; its matter and

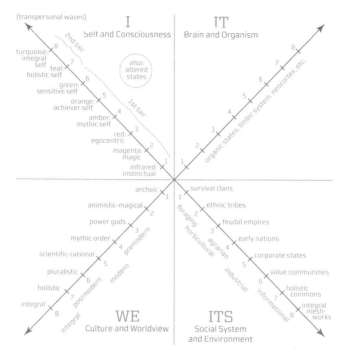

Figure 7. *Quadrants Focused on Humans.*

energy; and its concrete body—for all those are items that can be referred to in some sort of objective, **3ʳᵈ-person**, or "it" fashion.

That is what you or your organism looks like from the outside, in an objective-it stance, made of matter and energy and objects; whereas from the inside, you find not neurotransmitters but feelings, not limbic systems but intense desires, not a neocortex but inward visions, not matter-energy but consciousness, all described in **1st-person** immediateness. Which of those views is right? Both of them, according to the integral approach. They are two different views of the same occasion, namely you. The problems start when you try to deny or dismiss either of those perspectives. All 4 quadrants need to be included in any integral view.

The connections continue. Notice that every "I" is in relationship with other I's, which means that every "I" is a member of numerous we's. These "we's" represent not just *individual* but *group* (or *collective*) consciousness, not just subjective but intersubjective awareness—or **culture** in the broadest sense. This is represented in the **Lower-Left quadrant**. Likewise, every "we" has an exterior, or what it looks like from the outside, and this is the **Lower-Right quadrant**. The Lower Left is often called the **cultural** dimension (or the inside awareness of the group—its worldview, its shared values, shared feelings, and so forth), and the Lower Right the **social** dimension (or the exterior forms and behaviors of the group, which are studied by 3rd-person sciences such as systems theory).

Again, the quadrants are simply the **inside** and the **outside** of the **individual** and the **collective**, and the point is that all 4 quadrants need to be included if we want to be as integral as possible.

A Tour through the Quadrants

We are now at a point where we can start to put all the integral pieces together: quadrants, levels, lines, states, and types. So let's take a tour through the quadrants, tying all 5 elements together into an integral whole. And let's start with **levels** or **stages**.

All 4 quadrants show growth, development, or evolution. That is, they all show some sort of stages or levels of development, not as rigid rungs in a ladder but as fluid and flowing

waves of unfolding. This happens everywhere in the natural world, just as an oak unfolds from an acorn through stages of growth and development, or a Siberian tiger grows from a fertilized egg to an adult organism in exquisitely patterned stages of growth and development.

Likewise with humans in certain important ways. We have already seen several of these stages as they apply to humans. In the Upper Left or "I," for example, the self unfolds from egocentric to ethnocentric to worldcentric, or *body* to *mind* to *spirit*. In the Upper Right, felt energy phenomenologically expands from *gross* to *subtle* to *causal*. In the Lower Left, the "we" expands from *egocentric* ("me") to *ethnocentric* ("us") to *worldcentric* ("all of us"). This expansion of group awareness allows social systems—in the Lower Right—to expand from simple groups to more complex systems like nations and eventually even to global systems. These 3 simple stages in each of the quadrants are represented in figure 8 (p. 76).

Let's move from **levels** to **lines**. Developmental lines or streams occur in all 4 quadrants, but because we are focusing on personal development, we can look at how some of these lines appear in the Upper-Left quadrant. As we saw, there are over a dozen different multiple intelligences or developmental lines. Some of the more important include:

- the **cognitive** line (or awareness of what is)

- the **moral** line (awareness of what should be)

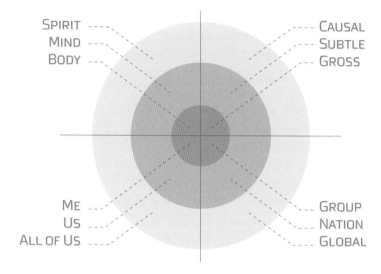

SPIRIT
MIND
BODY

CAUSAL
SUBTLE
GROSS

ME
US
ALL OF US

GROUP
NATION
GLOBAL

Figure 8. *AQAL.*

- **emotional** or **affective** line (the full spectrum of emotions)

- the **interpersonal** line (how I socially relate to others)

- the **needs** line (such as Maslow's needs hierarchy)

- the **self-identity** line (or "who am I?," such as Loevinger's ego development)

- the **aesthetic** line (or the line of self-expression, beauty, art, and felt meaning)

- the **psychosexual** line, which in its broadest sense means the entire spectrum of Eros (gross to subtle to causal)

- the **spiritual** line (where "spirit" is viewed not just as Ground, and not just as the highest stage, but as its own line of unfolding)

- the **values** line (or what a person considers most important, a line studied by Clare Graves and made popular by Spiral Dynamics)

All of those developmental lines or streams can move through the basic levels or stages. All of them can be included in the psychograph. If we use maps such as Robert Kegan's, Jane Loevinger's, or Clare Graves's, then we would have 5, 8, or even more levels or waves of development with which we could follow the natural unfolding of developmental lines or streams. Again, it is not a matter of which of them is right or wrong; it is a matter of how much "granularity" or "complexity" you need to more adequately understand a given situation.

We already gave one diagram of a psychograph (fig. 3). Figure 9 is another, taken from a Notre Dame business school presentation that uses the AQAL model in teaching integral leadership.

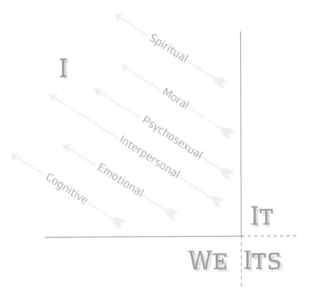

Figure 9. *Another Version of the Psychograph.*

As noted, all of the quadrants have developmental lines. We just focused on those in the Upper Left. In the Upper-Right quadrant, when it comes to humans, one of the most important is the bodily matter-energy line, which runs, as we saw, from gross energy to subtle energy to causal energy. As a developmental sequence, this refers to the permanent acquisition of a capacity to consciously master these energetic components of your being (otherwise, they appear merely as temporary states). The Upper-Right quadrant also refers to all of the exterior **behavior**, actions, and movements of my objective body (gross, subtle, or causal).

In the Lower-Left quadrant, cultural development itself often unfolds in waves, moving from what the pioneering genius Jean Gebser called *archaic* to *magic* to *mythic* to *mental* to *integral* and higher. In the Lower-Right quadrant, systems theory investigates the collective social systems that evolve (and that, in humans, include stages such as *foraging* to *agrarian* to *industrial* to *informational* systems). In figure 8, we simplified this to "group, nation, and global," but the general idea is simply that of unfolding levels of greater social complexity that are integrated into wider systems.

Again, for this simple overview, details are not as important as a general grasp of the unfolding or *flowering nature of all 4 quadrants*, which can include expanding spheres of consciousness, care, culture, and nature. In short, the "I" and the "we" and the "it" can evolve. Self and culture and nature can all develop and evolve, in an almost infinite number of waves and streams, reaching from atoms to supernovas, cells to Gaia, dust to Divinity.

If we understand their limitations, diagrams can often help here, and we already have seen perhaps the simplest diagram of AQAL (or IOS), which is figure 8, depicting just quadrants and levels. Figure 10 is a somewhat fuller version of figure 8, showing quadrants, levels, and lines. (Figure 10, by the way, is from one that is used by UNICEF to analyze worldwide patterns of children's hunger.)

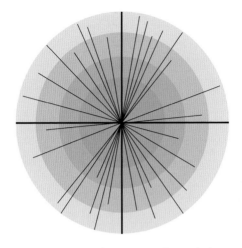

Figure 10. *Quadrants, Levels, and Lines.*

A variation on the UNICEF mandala is shown in figure 11, where the "lines" are depicted as "spirals," which indicates the spiraling nature of many developmental lines. But however depicted—lines, spirals, or streams—all 4 quadrants are overflowing with them.

If you have a general understanding of these simple diagrams, the rest is fairly easy, and we can now quickly finish with the other components. **States** occur in all quadrants (from weather states to states of consciousness). We focused on **states of consciousness** in the Upper Left (waking, dreaming, sleeping), and on **energetic states** in the Upper Right

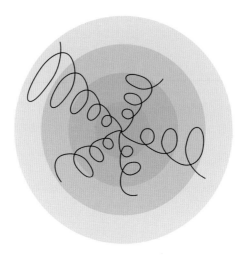

Figure 11. *Spiraling Streams and Waves.*

(gross, subtle, causal). Of course, if any of those become permanent acquisitions, they have become stages, not states.

There are **types** in all of the quadrants, too, but we focused on *masculine* and *feminine* types as they appear in
individuals. The masculine principle identifies more with
agency and the feminine identifies more with communion,
but the point is that every person has both of these components. Finally, as was saw, there is an **unhealthy type** of
masculine and feminine at all available stages—sick boy and
sick girl at all waves.

Seem complicated? In a sense it is. But in another sense,

the extraordinary complexity of humans and their relation to the universe can be simplified enormously by touching bases with the **quadrants** (the fact that every event can be looked at as an I, we, or it); **developmental lines** (or multiple intelligences), all of which move through **developmental levels** (from body to mind to spirit); with **states** and **types** at each of those levels.

That **Integral Model**—"all quadrants, all levels, all lines, all states, all types"—is the simplest model that can handle all of the truly essential items. We sometimes shorten all of that to simply "all quadrants, all levels"—or **AQAL**—where the quadrants are, for example, self, culture, and nature, and the levels are body, mind, and spirit, so we say that the Integral Approach involves **the cultivation of body, mind, and spirit in self, culture, and nature**.

Let's conclude what might be called this "Introduction to IOS Basic" by giving a few quick examples of its applications, or **"apps"**—in medicine, business, spirituality, ecology, and your individual life. This is where, I hope, you will start to see the Integral Model really come alive. . . .

chapter

4

HERE'S HOW IT WORKS: IOS APPS

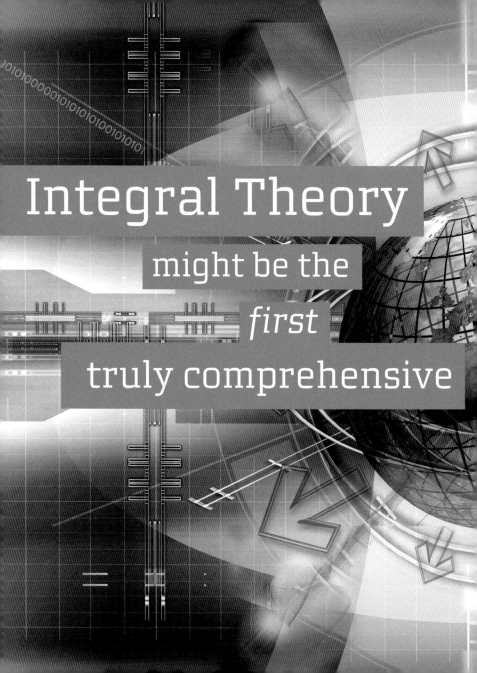

Integral Theory

might be the

first

truly comprehensive

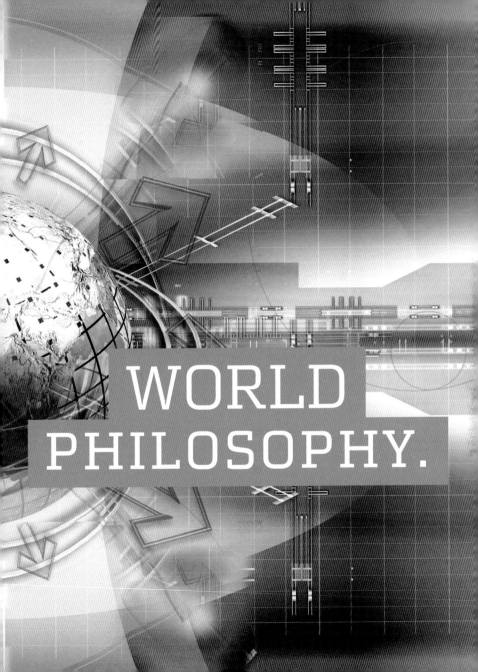

WORLD PHILOSOPHY.

But what does the Integral

Vision

look like on the ground–

in action?

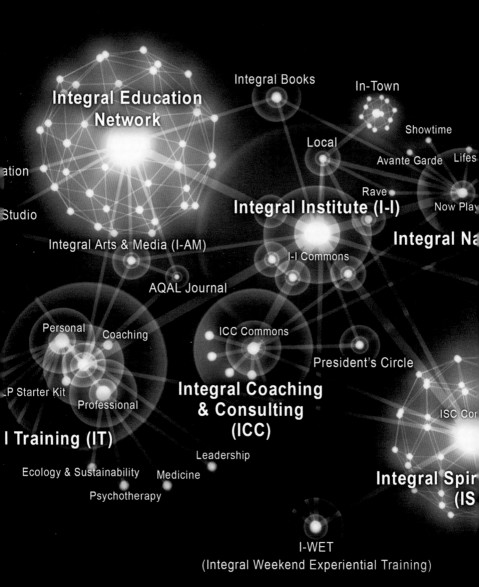

Integral Books

In-Town

Showtime

ation

Integral Education
Network

Local

Avante Garde Lifes

Studio

Integral Institute (I-I)

Rave

Now Play

Integral Na

Integral Arts & Media (I-AM)

I-I Commons

AQAL Journal

Personal Coaching

ICC Commons

President's Circle

-P Starter Kit

Professional

Integral Coaching
& Consulting
(ICC)

ISC Cor

I Training (IT)

Leadership

Ecology & Sustainability Medicine

Psychotherapy

Integral Spir
(IS

I-WET
(Integral Weekend Experiential Training)

Around the world, thousands of people are applying the Integral Vision in dozens of different fields, from art to ecology, medicine to criminology, business to personal transformation. Because an Integral framework explicitly harnesses and includes more truth, and more potentials, than any other approach, it makes one's work in any area radically more effective and fulfilling.

Integral Medicine

Nowhere is the Integral Model more immediately applicable than in medicine, and it is being increasingly adopted by health-care practitioners around the world. A quick trip through the quadrants will show why the Integral Model can be helpful. (See figure 12, p. 95.)

Orthodox or conventional medicine is a classic **Upper-Right quadrant** approach. It deals almost entirely with the physical organism using physical interventions: surgery, drugs, medication, and behavioral modification. Orthodox medicine believes essentially in the physical causes of physical illness, and therefore prescribes mostly physical interventions. But the Integral Model claims that every physical event (UR) has at least 4 dimensions (the quadrants), and thus even physical illness must be looked at from all 4 quadrants (not to mention levels, which we will address later). The integral model does not claim the Upper-Right quadrant is not important, only that it is, as it were, only one-fourth of the story.

The recent explosion of interest in alternative care—not to mention such disciplines as psychoneuroimmunology—has made it quite clear that the person's *interior states* (their emotions, psychological attitude, imagery, and intentions) play a crucial role in both the *cause* and the *cure* of even physical illness. In other words, the **Upper-Left quadrant** is a key

IOS APPS CASE STUDY #1:
integral medicine

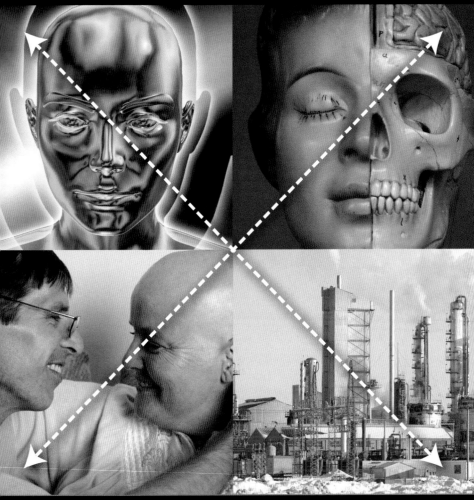

Factors in all four quadrants affect the cause/cure of an illness.

ingredient in any comprehensive medical care. Visualization, affirmation, and conscious use of imagery have empirically been shown to play a significant role in the management of most illnesses, and outcomes have been shown to depend on emotional states and mental outlook.

But as important as those subjective factors are, individual consciousness does not exist in a vacuum; it exists inextricably embedded in shared cultural values, beliefs, and worldviews. How a culture (LL) views a particular illness—with care and compassion or derision and scorn—can have a profound impact on how an individual copes with that illness (UL), which can directly affect the course of the physical illness itself (UR). The **Lower-Left quadrant** includes all of those enormous number of *intersubjective* factors that are crucial in any human interaction—such as the shared communication between doctor and patient; the attitudes of family and friends and how they are conveyed to the patient; the cultural acceptance (or derogation) of the particular illness (e.g., AIDS); and the very values of the culture that the illness itself threatens. All of those factors are to some degree causative in any physical illness and cure (simply because *every* occasion has 4 quadrants).

Of course, in practice, this quadrant needs to be limited to those factors that can be effectively engaged—perhaps doctor and patient communication skills, family and friends support groups, and a general understanding of cultural judgments and their effects on illness. Studies consistently show,

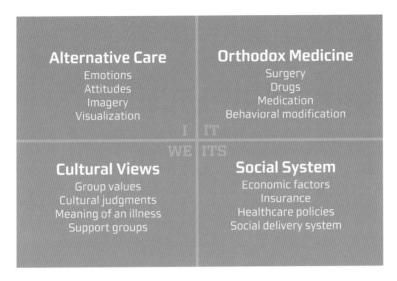

Figure 12. *Four Quadrants of Integral Medicine.*

for example, that cancer patients in support groups live longer than those without similar cultural support. Some of the more relevant factors from the Lower-Left quadrant are thus crucial in any comprehensive medical care.

The **Lower-Right quadrant** concerns all those material, economic, and social factors that are almost never counted as part of the disease entity, but in fact—like every other quadrant—are *causative* in both disease and cure. A social system that cannot deliver food will kill you (as famine-wracked countries demonstrate daily, alas). In the real world, where every entity has all 4 quadrants, a virus in the UR quadrant might be the focal issue, but without a social system (LR) that can deliver treatment, you will die. That is not a separate issue; it is central to the issue, because all occasions have 4 quadrants. The Lower-Right quadrant includes factors such as economics, insurance, social delivery systems, and even things as simple as how a hospital room is physically laid out (does it allow ease of movement, access to visitors, etc.?)—not to mention items like environmental toxins. The foregoing items refer to the "all-quadrant" aspect of the cause and management of illness. The "all-level" part refers to the fact that individuals have—at least—physical, emotional, mental, and spiritual *levels* in each of those quadrants (see fig. 8). Some illnesses have largely physical causes and physical cures (get hit by a bus, break your leg). But most illnesses have causes and cures that include *emotional*, *mental*, and *spiritual* components. Literally hundreds of researchers from around the world have added immeasurably to our understanding of the "multi-level" nature of disease and cure (including invaluable additions from the great wisdom traditions, shamanic to Tibetan Buddhist). The point is simply that by adding these levels to the quadrants, a much more comprehensive—and effective—medical model begins to emerge.

In short, a truly effective and comprehensive medical plan would be all-quadrant, all-level: the idea is simply that each quadrant or dimension (fig. 5, p. 70)—I, we, and it—has physical, emotional, mental, and spiritual levels or waves (fig. 8,

p. 76), and a truly integral treatment would take all of these realities into account. Not only is this type of integral treatment more *effective*, it is for that reason more *cost-efficient*—which is why even organizational medicine is looking at it more closely.

(If you're interested in learning more about this approach, see the Integral Medicine Center at www.integrallife.com.)

Integral Business

Applications of the Integral Model have recently exploded in business and leadership, because the applications are so immediate and obvious. The quadrants (fig. 13, p. 98) give the 4 "environments" or "markets" in which a product must survive, and the levels give the types of values that will be both producing and buying the product. Research into the values hierarchy—such as Maslow's and Graves's (e.g., Spiral Dynamics), which have already had an enormous influence on business—can be combined with the quadrants (which show how these levels of values appear in the 4 different environments)—to give a truly comprehensive map of the marketplace (which covers both traditional markets and cybermarkets).

Moreover, Integral Leadership training programs, based

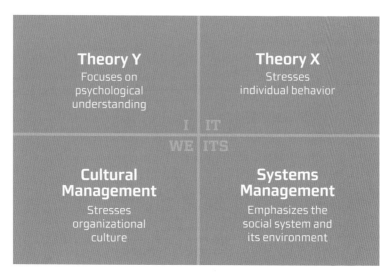

Figure 13. *Four Quadrants of Integral Business.*

on an integral or AQAL model, have also begun to flourish. There are today 4 major theories of business management (Theory X, which stresses individual behavior; Theory Y, which focuses on psychological understanding; cultural management, which stresses organizational culture; and systems management, which emphasizes the social system and its governance). Those 4 management theories are in fact the 4 quadrants, and an Integral Approach would necessarily include all 4 approaches. Add levels and lines, and an incredibly rich and sophisticated model of leadership emerges, which is easily the most comprehensive available today.

integral business

(If you would like to pursue this approach, please see the Integral Leadership and Business Center at www .integrallife.com.)

Integral Ecology

Integral or AQAL ecology has already been pioneered by several associates at Integral Institute, and promises to revolutionize both how we think about environmental issues and how we pragmatically address and remedy them.

The basic idea is simple: anything less than an integral or comprehensive approach to environmental issues is doomed to failure. Both the interior (or Left-Hand) and the exterior (or Right-Hand) quadrants need to be taken into account. **Exterior** environmental sustainability is clearly needed; but without a growth and development in the **interior** domains to worldcentric levels of values and consciousness, the environment remains gravely at risk. Those focusing only on exterior solutions are contributing to the problem. Self, culture, and nature must be liberated together or not at all. How to do so is the focus of Integral Ecology.

(If you are interested in a more integral approach to ecology, the environment, and sustainability, please join us at the Integral Ecology Center at www.integrallife.com).

Relational and Socially Engaged Spirituality

The major implication of an AQAL approach to spirituality is that physical, emotional, mental, and spiritual levels of being should be simultaneously exercised in self, culture, and nature (i.e., in the I, we, and it domains). There are many variations on this theme, ranging from socially engaged spirituality to relationships as spiritual path, and we include all of those important contributions in Integral Life Practice (see chap. 6). The implications of an Integral Spirituality are profound and widespread, and just beginning to have an impact.

But before we can fully understand what "integral spirituality" means, we must understand the meaning of "spirituality" itself. And here we run into a thicket of problems. But the integral approach claims to have made sense of all of them. Does it?

Shall we see?

chapter

5

IS THIS YOU? ⬇
"SPIRITUAL BUT NOT RELIGIOUS"

Why is it that **religion** is such a **complex, confusing,** and **polarizing** **force** in the world?

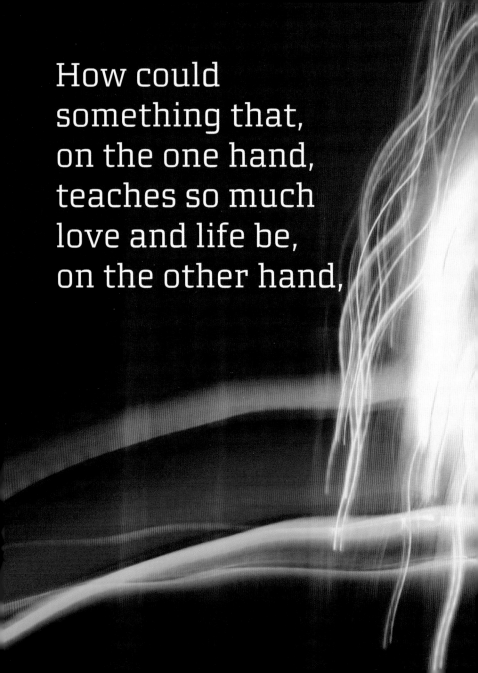

How could
something that,
on the one hand,
teaches so much
love and life be,
on the other hand,

the cause
of so much
death and destruction?

Glib answers won't work here. This is perhaps the most serious issue any person—or the world itself, for that matter—will ever face. The Integral Approach is known for "making sense of everything." Can it help make sense of this? Definitely. But I'll warn you right now, it's tricky because what people call "spirituality" has at least 5 very different meanings, referring variously to quadrants, levels, lines, states, and types. But if you take that into account—if you take an AQAL view—there is a place for virtually all of the different approaches to this topic, and the entire thing starts to make sense. If you don't, the overall topic of spirituality makes virtually no sense whatsoever. But put it all together, and you can indeed begin to "make sense of everything." Shall we give it a go?

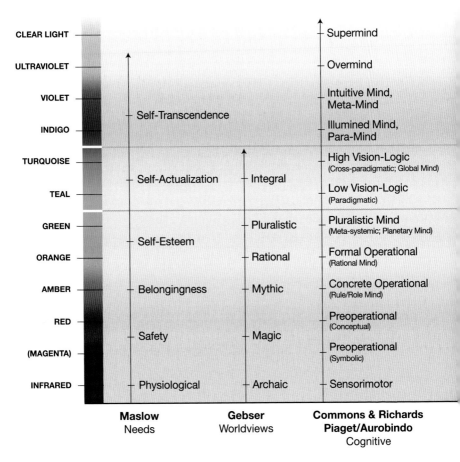

	CLEAR LIGHT			Supermind
	ULTRAVIOLET			Overmind
	VIOLET	Self-Transcendence		Intuitive Mind, Meta-Mind
	INDIGO			Illumined Mind, Para-Mind
	TURQUOISE	Self-Actualization	Integral	High Vision-Logic (Cross-paradigmatic; Global Mind)
	TEAL			Low Vision-Logic (Paradigmatic)
	GREEN	Self-Esteem	Pluralistic	Pluralistic Mind (Meta-systemic; Planetary Mind)
	ORANGE		Rational	Formal Operational (Rational Mind)
	AMBER	Belongingness	Mythic	Concrete Operational (Rule/Role Mind)
	RED	Safety	Magic	Preoperational (Conceptual)
	(MAGENTA)			Preoperational (Symbolic)
	INFRARED	Physiological	Archaic	Sensorimotor
		Maslow Needs	**Gebser** Worldviews	**Commons & Richards Piaget/Aurobindo** Cognitive

Figure 14. *Some Major Developmental Lines.*

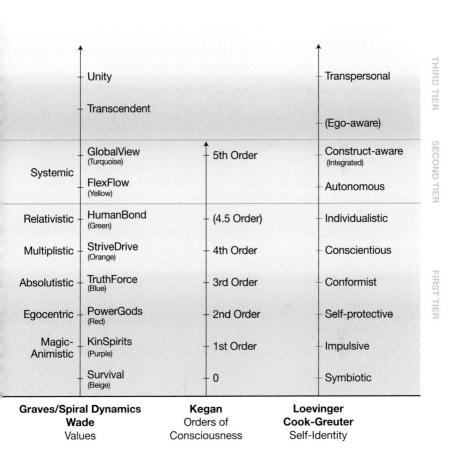

	Graves/Spiral Dynamics Wade	Kegan	Loevinger Cook-Greuter	
	Unity		Transpersonal	THIRD TIER
	Transcendent		(Ego-aware)	
Systemic	GlobalView (Turquoise)	5th Order	Construct-aware (Integrated)	SECOND TIER
	FlexFlow (Yellow)		Autonomous	
Relativistic	HumanBond (Green)	(4.5 Order)	Individualistic	FIRST TIER
Multiplistic	StriveDrive (Orange)	4th Order	Conscientious	
Absolutistic	TruthForce (Blue)	3rd Order	Conformist	
Egocentric	PowerGods (Red)	2nd Order	Self-protective	
Magic-Animistic	KinSpirits (Purple)	1st Order	Impulsive	
	Survival (Beige)	0	Symbiotic	

**Graves/Spiral Dynamics
Wade**
Values

Kegan
Orders of
Consciousness

**Loevinger
Cook-Greuter**
Self-Identity

Rainbow Waves and Shimmering Streams

Let's start with the Upper-Left quadrant, or the interior of an individual, and look more closely at this fascinating phenomenon of multiple intelligences (or developmental lines). We already saw that each of us possesses at least a dozen major developmental lines, including needs, values, cognition, morals, and self. Each of these has been investigated by numerous developmentalists. Figure 14 is a psychograph summarizing the results of a few of the best known and most highly respected of these researchers.

To begin with, you might notice that the levels or waves of consciousness are represented with colors of the rainbow. This is a common practice in the wisdom traditions, and it allows us to discuss levels in a very general and, well, colorful way. The rainbow simply represents vertical **altitude**—or the degree of development (the degree of consciousness or complexity) of any line. This also allows us easily to compare the various levels in numerous different developmental lines, by seeing which are at the same rainbow altitude. This is what figure 14 does, for example. (Don't worry about some of the intermediary colors, like amber or teal—they were selected so as to fit with several models that also use colors. The basic idea is as simple as a rainbow of colors representing a spectrum of consciousness. . . .)

To the far left of the diagram is one of the better-known developmental lines, that of Maslow's needs hierarchy, which means . . .

Well, perhaps we should stop right here and deal first with the enormous misconceptions surrounding the word "hierarchy." For so many people, this has become a very dirty word, and for understandable reasons. But there are at least two very different types of hierarchy, which researchers call oppressive hierarchies (or dominator hierarchies) and growth hierarchies (or actualization hierarchies). A *dominator hierarchy* is just that, a ranking system that dominates, exploits, and represses people. The most notorious of these are the caste systems East and West. Any hierarchy is a dominator hierarchy if it subverts individual or collective growth.

Actualization hierarchies, on the other hand, are the actual means of growth itself. Far from causing oppression, they are how you end it. Growth or developmental hierarchies classically move, in humans, from egocentric to ethnocentric to worldcentric to Kosmocentric* waves. In the natural world, growth hierarchies are everywhere, the most common being the unfolding from atoms to molecules to cells

---

* *Kosmocentric* means *third-tier oriented*. It's from the beautiful Greek word *Kosmos,* which means the *total* universe of matter, body, mind, and spirit (and not just its pitifully lowest level of matter, which is what "cosmos" has sadly come to mean . . .).

to organisms. Growth hierarchies are always nested hierarchies, which means that each higher level *transcends and includes* its predecessors. Organisms transcend and include cells, which transcend and include molecules, which transcend and include atoms, which transcend and include quarks, and so on. In a growth hierarchy, higher levels don't oppress lower levels, they embrace them! They literally include them, they envelop them. Each level in a growth hierarchy is indeed ranked in a higher-archy, because it represents an *increase* in the capacity for care, consciousness, cognition, morals, and so on. Growth is a *development* that is *envelopment*—egocentric to ethnocentric to worldcentric to Kosmocentric. All of the hierarchies shown in figure 14 are growth hierarchies, or various streams flowing through waves of increasing embrace.

In short, dominator hierarchies cause oppression, growth hierarchies end it. (Can you see why it is such a disaster when *all* hierarchies are condemned?)

So let's return to Maslow's needs hierarchy (fig. 15). Abraham Maslow's meticulous research showed that individuals tend to move through a growth sequence of **needs**. As each lower need is met or fulfilled, a higher need tends to emerge. *Physiological needs* are the simplest—those for food, shelter, and basic biological necessities. If those needs are met, then an individual sense of self begins to emerge with its self-protection and *safety needs*. If those are met, the individual seeks not just safety but *belongingness*. Once a sense

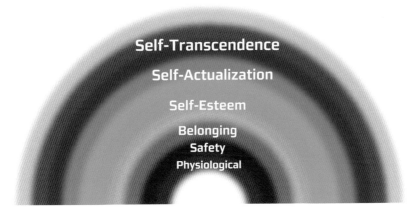

Figure 15. *Maslow's Needs Hierarchy (Holarchy).*

of belongingness is secured, individuals tend to be motivated by the newly emerging *self-esteem needs*. If those are fulfilled, even higher needs of the self begin to emerge, which Maslow called *self-actualization needs*. And if those are met, individuals tend to be motivated by *self-transcendence needs*, or the needs not just to fulfill the self but move beyond it altogether into higher, deeper, and wider circles and waves of care and consciousness, some of which start to look decidedly transpersonal or spiritual.

Probably the most famous of the developmental sequences is that of Jean Gebser, which moves from **archaic** to **magic** to **mythic** to **rational** to **pluralistic** to **integral**. The great thing about Gebser's stages is that they mean pretty much exactly what they sound like they mean. (I've divided his highest stage into two, which helps.) And as Gebser himself pointed out, his "integral stage" is actually just the opening to higher (or "super-integral" and transpersonal) stages.

We can especially see this if we look at the developmental stream of **cognition**, or the capacity for awareness and perspectives. The cognitive line shown in figure 14 is an amalgam of the important research of Michael Commons & Francis Richards, Jean Piaget, and Sri Aurobindo, indicating that cognition unfolds from the **sensory mind** to the **concrete mind** to the **formal mind** to the **higher mind** to the **illumined mind** to the **intuitive mind** to the **overmind** and **supermind**. Notice again how the very highest stages start to look transpersonal or spiritual.

Next we can look at the work of Clare Graves, on what he called **value systems**, and its popularization in a model called Spiral Dynamics (created by Don Beck and Christopher Cowan). At the *magic-animistic* stage, values are indeed "magical" and "animistic," with elemental forces magically ruling the world. At the *egocentric* stage, the power drives come front and center; one's values are those centered on "me" and "my power." With *absolutistic values*, one's values move from "me" to "us," or from egocentric to ethnocentric, and are believed to be given by an eternal source that is absolutely and rigidly true for everybody (whether the Bible,

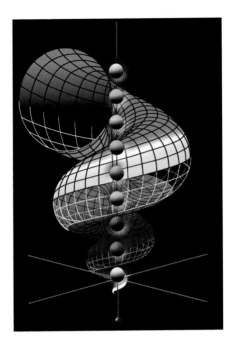

An artist's conception of Spiral Dynamics and its major levels of values development. (Artists: Ben Wright and Ken Wilber)

the Koran, or Chairman Mao's Little Red Book); violating them will result in temporal and possibly eternal damnation. This is often referred to as "mythic-membership," because if you don't believe the ethnocentric myths, you are in deep trouble.

As development moves from mythic conformist to the next stage, one's values switch from ethnocentric to the beginning of worldcentric, which Graves called the switch from absolutistic to *multiplistic*, meaning that there are multiple ways to view reality, not just one rigidly correct way. This results in a switch from **traditional values** to **modern values**. This differentiation continues into the next stage, which Graves called *relativistic*, because not only is there a multitude of different beliefs, they are all relative, which results in a typically *postmodern* and *pluralistic* worldview. This view is so pluralistic, in fact, that it often ends up completely fragmented and alienated, drenched in nihilism, irony, and meaninglessness (sound familiar?). It is only at the next stage, the *systemic*, that a truly integrated and cohesive worldview can finally begin to emerge, which allows the start of what one sociologist called the **Integral Age**. Clare Graves called it the switch from first-tier values (marked by their partiality) to second-tier values (marked by their integrated nature).

Clare Graves was one of the researchers who first discovered the incredibly important difference between the **first tier** and **second tier** of development. What is this extraordinary difference? All of the stages in first tier believe firmly that their values are the only true and correct values; everybody else's are deeply confused. But starting with the leap to second tier—or the beginning of the truly integral levels—it is understood that all of the other values and stages are correct in their own ways, or are appropriate for their own levels. Second tier makes room for all of the other values, and begins to pull them all together and integrate them into larger tapestries of care and inclusivity.

In many ways, this is the same thing that Abe Maslow previously found in the leap from the **deficiency needs** (of lack and scarcity) to the **being needs** (of self-actualization and self-transcendence), and, in fact, Graves was attempting to make sense of this finding of Maslow's. The developmental leap from first tier to second tier is a leap from fragmentation and alienation to wholeness and integration, from nihilism and irony to deep meaning and value.

This integral development continues into the **third tier** (or "super-integral" and suprapersonal) waves, two of which Jenny Wade, in her extension of the Graves system, calls *transpersonal* and then *unitive*.

All told, one's values grow and develop from **tribal** to **traditional** to **modern** to **postmodern** to **integral** and **super-integral**, on the way to even higher unfoldings in the evolutionary future. Today, in our culture as a whole, we stand right on the brink of the extraordinary leap from first to second tier, from postmodern to integral . . . a leap we will come back to shortly.

Robert Kegan's work on **orders of consciousness** is probably some of the most widely respected anywhere. As is the sophisticated theory and research of Jane Loevinger on the **stages of self development**. You can see both of these in figure 14.

One of Loevinger's main students and successors, Susann Cook-Greuter, has done significant research on the highest or third-tier levels of self development, which are also listed in figure 14. (By the way, Robert Kegan, Don Beck, and Susann Cook-Greuter are all founding members of Integral Institute.) Don't worry if all the labels on this figure don't make sense; all of our points can be made very simply using the information you already have.

For now, you might simply notice, looking at all the streams in figures 9 and 10, that, in general, the first tier of growth involves moving from *prepersonal* to *personal* development; the second tier involves *integrated* personal development (and the beginning of the "integral" stages); and the third tier involves *transpersonal* development (or the beginning of "super-integral" stages).

Thus, overall evolution and development moves from prepersonal to personal to transpersonal, from subconscious to self-conscious to superconscious, from pre-rational to rational to trans-rational, from preconventional to conventional to postconventional, from id to ego to Spirit. With third-tier or transpersonal development, one's self begins to expand beyond the personal realm and into a realm of vast spaciousness, luminous clarity, and unitive experiences, all of which have a decidedly spiritual flavor. But unlike the magic and mythic levels, which are mere concepts and dogmatic beliefs, these are levels of direct experience and immediate awareness.

The Pre/Post Fallacy

So let's stop and note that fact: researchers have found that the very *highest* stages of cognitive, moral, and self growth all take on a transpersonal or spiritual tone. Let's call this "**highest-level spirituality**," and put that down as one of the important meanings of "spiritual." (We will also refer to this aspect of spirituality as **trans-rational** and **transpersonal spirituality**.)

But let's also note a strange, fascinating item: some of the trans-rational and transpersonal stages superficially resemble some of the pre-rational and prepersonal stages.

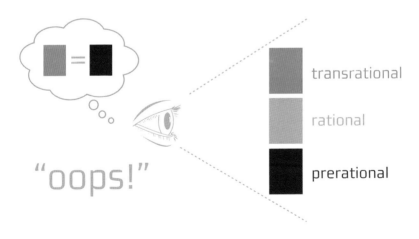

Because *pre*-conventional stages and *post*-conventional stages are *both non*-conventional, they are confused and even equated by the untutored eye. Pre-rational stages are confused with trans-rational stages simply because both are nonrational; pre-egoic stages are confused with trans-egoic simply because both are non-egoic; transverbal is confused with preverbal because both are nonverbal, and so on.

This confusion is known as *the pre/trans fallacy* (or *the pre/post fallacy*). Once it occurs, people make one of two big mistakes. They either reduce all trans-rational realities to pre-rational childish twaddle (think Freud), or they elevate pre-rational childish images and myths to trans-rational glory (think Jung). Both reductionism and elevationism have plagued the discussion of spirituality from the beginning, and so one of the first things that a truly Integral approach contributes is a way out of that particular nightmare.

A Pre-Rational Mythic God and a Trans-Rational Unitive Spirit

At the very least, it behooves us to recognize that there are, based upon significant scientific and empirical research, stages of development that involve prerational, childish, preconventional, narcissistic fantasy, and those that involve postconventional, trans-rational, ego-aware, post-autonomous, transpersonal awareness. In the former (e.g., magical-animistic, mythic-membership), ultimate reality is indeed pictured as a white-haired, grey-bearded gentleman in the sky, or somebody who walks on water and is born from a biological virgin, or an elderly sage who was 900 years old at birth, and so on. All of these pre-rational myths are taken to be literally and concretely true. But in the latter or postconventional stages, ultimate reality is pictured as a nondual ground of being, a state of timeless presence, or a post-rational (not pre-rational and not anti-rational) state of unity consciousness. The difference between the two is indeed night and day, with the dawn of reason separating them.

If we put all of the scientific research on human development together, it appears that there are indeed at least these three broad arcs of human psychological growth: prepersonal to personal to transpersonal, or pre-rational to rational to trans-rational, or subconscious to self-conscious to super-conscious. Each of the stages in those arcs continues to **transcend and include** its predecessor(s). As each new level **unfolds**, it **enfolds** its predecessor—a development that is envelopment—so that the cumulative effect is integral indeed, just as with atoms to molecules to cells to organisms. Nothing is lost, all is retained, in the extraordinary unfolding and enfolding, developing and enveloping, transcending and including, negating and preserving, that is consciousness evolution.

We are not, at this point, talking about whether there is or is not a "real" Spirit or an actual Ground of Being. We are talking about whether there are these three great arcs (or, sliced a slightly different way, three great tiers) of human development, and the answer is that any empirical study that has looked carefully at the entire sweep of human development has concluded **yes**. Those who deny the stages of superconscious and transpersonal awareness are simply and absolutely denying the scientific evidence. And frankly, we are no more obliged to take their views into account than we are to take seriously the churchmen who refused to look through Galileo's telescope because they already "knew" what they would see.

So, if we now move to that most fascinating of all questions and do indeed ask if there is, or is not, an actual Ground of Being, a genuine Spirit, a real Godhead underlying all phenomena, who better to ask than those individuals who are at the higher or highest levels—the transpersonal levels—of development? And if we do ask them, what do they say?

Well, let's start by repeating that each of these three great arcs has its idea of what ultimate reality is. We saw that in the first arc, leading up to rationality, ultimate reality is viewed as **magic** and **mythic** in nature. Here, to be honest, perhaps 80% of the tenets of the world's major religions can be found, Shinto to Christian to Islamic to Hebraic to Hindu to Buddhist to Taoist. This includes much New Age magic.

Then human development enters a period that appears to

be non-religious and even anti-religious, namely, all of the stages of the second major arc, the arc of Person and Reason. Rational science here comes to the fore, bringing with it an extraordinary boon for humankind in terms of reduction of suffering and increase in longevity. Counting disease, hunger, illness, and infant mortality, rational science has alleviated more actual human suffering than all of the prerational mythic religions combined. That science can be misused is not the issue; its positive gains are staggering and undeniable.

Then, right when it looked like all things religious and spiritual were in our past, relics of archaic history, comes the third major arc. Building on the gains of rational awareness, development begins to transcend and include rationality in even larger circles of care and consciousness. Here, ultimate reality is seen not in anthropomorphic terms, which color the first arc, and not in rational terms, which color the second, but rather in terms of Being, Emptiness, Consciousness, and Suchness—terms such as a Ground of All Being; a universal Consciousness; a nondual Suchness or Is-ness; a vast, open, empty Luminous Clarity; a mirror-like Witnessing Awareness; a Godhead prior to any Trinity; a pure, infinite, transcendental, selfless Self; an unbounded, spacious, radiant, unobstructed and unqualifiable Consciousness as Such; a timeless, endless, eternal Presence or Now; a Thusness or Suchness or Is-ness of each and every moment, beyond any conceptualizations at all, but as simple and obvious as the person who is reading this page, or the sound of a robin singing, or the cool quench of the first swallow from a glass of iced tea on a hot summer's day.

This is not your father's religion, and not your mother's, and certainly not your grandparent's. And yet the vast majority of individuals who reach the stages of the third arc/tier report that reality is some version of an infinite/eternal Ground of All Being. But this transpersonal reality is *at the opposite end* of the spectrum of human development from the magic and mythic conceptions of the prepersonal and pre-rational arc. They are, indeed, as different as night and day, and we absolutely must, at the least, stop confusing them.

But the media, to give only the most obvious example, completely confuse pre and trans. Any transpersonal non-dual spirituality is unceremoniously lumped with, and dumped into, the prepersonal garbage pail. The only kinds of spirituality the media recognizes are all pre-rational.

(To make matters worse at that end, the press seems to recognize only two types of religion: fundamentalist nutcases and New Age nutcases. Both of those, of course, are *pre*-rational, with the fundamentalist believing in amber dogma and myth, the New Ager believing in magenta magic. Any transrational orientation, such as transpersonal psychology, is lumped in with the New-Age nutcases. But heck, the New Agers aren't taken seriously enough to think about. The only two people that the press knows who are "spiritual" are George W. Bush and Osama bin Laden. And the press can't figure out which is the more dangerous.)

The fact is, conservatives tend to support the first arc and liberals tend to support the second arc, with neither one of them even vaguely aware of the third arc. So the third arc is either dismissed entirely, or, as we said, subjected to a pre/trans fallacy and completely confused with the first arc.

Night and day indeed. So it's worth repeating that, at the very least, these two diametrically different kinds of "non-rational spirituality" (pre and trans) simply must be acknowledged, by the press, or at least by anybody who can read without moving their lips.

It looks very much as if the phrase "spiritual but not

religious" often applies to this third arc. And even if people who describe themselves that way are not permanently at these higher, transpersonal waves, many of them seem to be intuiting these higher realities. They do not want ego-centric magic or ethnocentric mythic religion, drenched in dogma and creed and conceptual beliefs. They want direct experience beyond words and concepts, a supramental, transrational, postconventional spirituality, with its imme-diate awareness and radiant consciousness. They are in-deed **spiritual but not religious**. And they do claim to be directly aware of a nondual, empty, open, spacious, infinite, unqualifiable Thusness, by whatever name you care to call that particular rose.

Again with the Pre/Post Fallacy

Excuse my French, but the ultimate bitch when it comes to "God" or "Spirit" or "Absolute Reality" is that the whole thing is caught in a staggeringly huge pre/post fallacy. The pre-rational and the trans-rational versions of spirituality sound similar or even identical to the untutored eye, simply because both are "nonrational," and hence they are treated as basically the same by anyone caught in this pre/trans fal-lacy, even though they are actually poles apart. And when night and day are confused, the trans-rational stages of Nondual Consciousness—which are, wherever they appear, said to disclose an ultimate Freedom and Fullness, a Great Liberation from alienation, fragmentation, and suffering—are thoroughly confused with the pre-rational stages of a mythic God—stages that have arguably caused more human-made suffering that any other factor in history. The means of our Liberation are confused with the cause of most of our misery. Then, in running from what appears to be the cause of suffering, we are running from our salvation.

This is, um, very bad. And this confusion is everywhere, not only in the press, but in the religions themselves and the culture at large. Yet it is stopped in its tracks by an IOS. Simply by looking at the "levels" aspect of AQAL, these incredibly important differences can be first, spotted, and second, utilized.

At the same time, let's be honest about the numbers involved here. Studies consistently show that around **70% of the world's population is at ethnocentric (or lower) levels of development**. That is, at or below mythic, amber, conformist.* Put yet another way, about 70% of the world's population are fundamentalists (or lower) in their spiritual orientation. About 30% are at the second arc (orange to turquoise). And less than 1% are stably at the transpersonal stages. But those transpersonal stages do exist, they are

* For amber altitude, see figure 14, page 112–113.

there, and they are open to any who want to take up a transformative practice, such as Integral Life Practice (ILP), in order to engage them. (For the details of an ILP, please see chap. 6.)

So that is the first meaning of "spirituality": the highest (or third-tier) levels in any of the lines. Now let's check in with lines themselves.

Spiritual Intelligence: Let's Check In with Lines

Less than 1% are stably at the third arc or tier?* Yup. Any way you slice it, not very many people, at this time in history, have grown and evolved into the transpersonal stages or waves of consciousness.

Does that mean that less than 1% of humanity are genuinely spiritual? Or, to say the same thing from a different angle, does that mean that you have to be at indigo or higher

---

* The third arc and the third tier refer to essentially the same stages, those that are transpersonal. Second tier and second arc are slightly different, in that "second tier" refers to levels that are the first to be integrative (namely, teal and turquoise), while "second arc" is broader and refers to levels that are personal (roughly, orange to turquoise). These are just different ways to group the same developmental levels.

in order to have any genuine spiritual awareness at all? Surely that isn't correct. Something seems wrong here.

And indeed, something is. What's wrong is that we haven't completed our AQAL sweep. We haven't finished looking at spirituality from all of the quadrants, levels, lines, states, and types. So let's look next at "lines." Is there a **spiritual line** of development? Is there a **spiritual intelligence**?

The answer is, almost certainly. In a ground-breaking series of research studies, James Fowler has mapped out some of the basic stages of the spiritual stream or line. So let's pause and look more carefully at this line. And while we are doing so, you might keep asking yourself: at what stage or wave am I in this important stream?

Here (below and in fig. 16) are Fowler's stages of spiritual intelligence, and notice right off that they are—no surprise—a variation on the general levels of archaic, magic, mythic, rational, pluralistic, integral (and super-integral). Those are simply some of the more common names for the rainbow or altitude of consciousness, and they naturally show a great similarity with the specific names of Fowler's stages.

Fowler's stages are:

0. preverbal, predifferentiated

1. projective-magical, 1st-person dominated

2. mythic-literal, concrete myths and stories

3. conventional, conformist, 2nd-person dominated

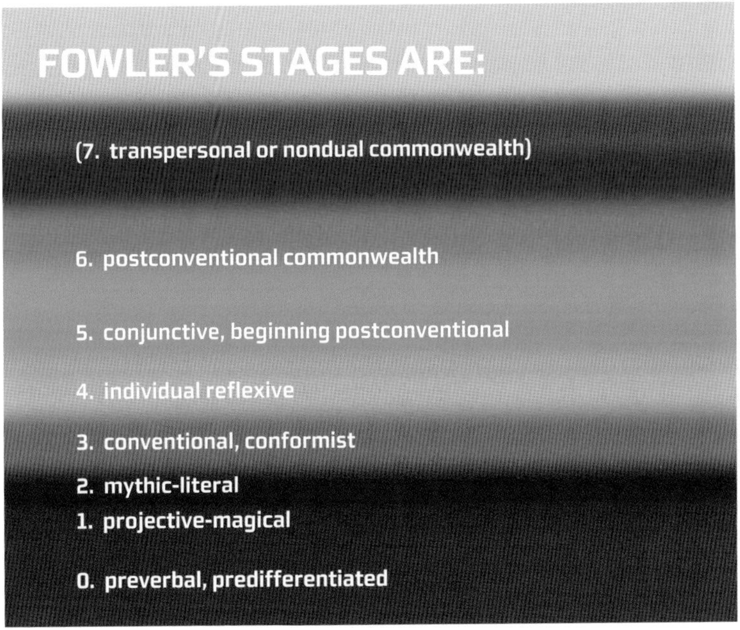

FOWLER'S STAGES ARE:

(7. transpersonal or nondual commonwealth)

6. postconventional commonwealth

5. conjunctive, beginning postconventional

4. individual reflexive

3. conventional, conformist

2. mythic-literal

1. projective-magical

0. preverbal, predifferentiated

Figure 16. *Fowler's Stages of Spiritual Intelligence.*

4. individual reflexive, beginning of 3rd-person

5. conjunctive, pluralistic, dialectical, multiculturally sensitive

6. postconventional, universal commonwealth

(7. transpersonal or nondual commonwealth)

I believe that the meanings of most of those are obvious, and we will define any new terms we need as we go along. The point is simply that, from the available evidence, it appears that you do NOT have to be at the very highest levels in any of the lines in order to possess some sort of spirituality. Not only are there altered states or peak experiences of authentic spirituality (which we will cover in a moment), spirituality it-self grows and develops through *every* level of conscious-ness, not just the highest. In other words, not only is there a *highest-level spirituality* (and, see below, an *altered-states spirituality*), there is a *developmental-line spirituality*, a **spiritual intelligence**.

This line, like most of the multiple intelligences, appears to begin somewhere in the earliest years. Even as an adult, you still might only be at stage 1 in your spiritual intelligence, but you are NEVER without some form of spiritual intelligence or spiritual awareness.

So what aspect or dimension of spirituality does spiritual intelligence refer to? How is that aspect of spirituality defined?

Different researchers have defined spiritual intelligence in different ways, based on the type of research and results they are dealing with. But perhaps the simplest and easiest involves the following. Paul Tillich said that "spiritual" refers to that which indicates a person's **ultimate concern**. At year one, your ultimate concern may be where to get food, but you are never without some sort of that awareness and meaning-investment. The human organism seems to have evolved, as one of its inherited multiple intelligences, the capacity or smarts for handling ultimate concern.

When it comes to this aspect or dimension of spirituality, everybody has religion. If you are at an orange level of the spiritual line—the individual-reflexive—you may have a very formal, rational version of ultimate concern, as when we say, "Logic is Spock's religion." But it is not something you are ever simply without. You can have:

- an archaic spirituality (food/sex fetish),

- a magic spirituality (voodoo, Santeria),

- a mythic spirituality (fundamentalism, mythic-membership God/Goddess),

- a rational spirituality (scientific materialism, logo-centrism),

- a pluralistic spirituality (postmodernism as the answer to everything, pluralitis),

- a systems spirituality (deep ecology, Gaiasophy),

- an integral and super-integral spirituality (AQAL),

and so on. Remember, in any of the multiple intelligences, the contents of any level in the line often vary dramatically from person to person and culture to culture.

The "level" part doesn't determine the specific content of one's ultimate concern, but simply the degree of development, complexity, and consciousness that goes into one's ultimate concern, whatever it is, at that level.

So: **what level of God do you believe in?** Is the food of your ultimate concern, the stuff of your ultimate reality, physical food, emotional food, mental food, transpersonal food? What is the altitude of your reality? How high is your God?

In short, *What do you worship?* Because it's definitely something. . . .

States and Stages

At this point, perhaps we can start to see how useful the AQAL model (or IOS) is for making sense of spirituality. Notice that even the two aspects of spirituality we have discussed thus far—highest-level spirituality and developmental-line spirituality—seem almost contradictory at points. For example, highest-level spirituality claims that children do not possess any authentic spirituality, whereas developmental-line spirituality claims that they do. (You would not believe the academic food fights that have been generated by that absolutely fruitless debate.)

Put that debate another way: We have seen that virtually

100% of people have a spiritual intelligence, and yet less than 1% are at the highest levels of that, or any, line. If by "spiritual" you mean "the highest levels of any line," then only the highest levels of the spiritual line are spiritual.

Get it? The identical word "spiritual" is used in two completely different ways. If we didn't explicitly spot this using an AQAL model (or something similar), we'd be completely contradictory and lost, or at least darned confused.

And the confusion would just be starting. There are other aspects of spirituality, or other ways that people commonly use the term "spirituality," other than levels and lines. For one thing, there are states of consciousness that appear spiritual, such as some **peak experiences**, **altered states**, **religious experiences**, and **meditative states**. And, indeed, this appears to be one of the most common ways that people think of spirituality. It is certainly something that we would not want to leave out of any inventory of religious or spiritual phenomena.

We have seen that virtually 100% of people have a spiritual intelligence and less than 1% of them are at the highest levels of that line. But what about states? How often do states occur? Well, when was the last time you got high?

Okay, sorry. Let's put it this way: research consistently shows that you can be at virtually any level or stage of growth and have profound and authentic religious experiences, peak experiences, or altered states. The way we put this in chapter 2 was: "The reason these peak experiences are possible is that many of the major states of consciousness (such as

NATURE
MYSTICISM

DEITY
MYSTICISM

FORMLESS
MYSTICISM

waking-gross, dreaming-subtle, and formless-causal) are ever-present possibilities." Like those natural states, certain religious or spiritual states seem to be ever-present, or at least ever-available.

What are some typical spiritual states or peak experiences in the waking state? A quite typical one is that you are walking in nature and you have a peak experience of being one with all of nature. Call that **nature mysticism**. What is a type of spiritual state or spiritual experience in the dream state? You might be dreaming of a great cloud of luminous, radiant love, and you might even feel that you are becoming one with that infinite love. Call that **deity mysticism**. With reference to the deep dreamless-formless state, is it possible to have a spiritual experience focused on that? It appears so, because some spiritual or religious experiences are described as empty, formless, unmanifest—the Void, Abyss, Ur-grund, Ayin, and so on. Call this **formless mysticism**. (We also call it *causal mysticism*, after the causal or formless state itself.) Finally, there are quite common experiences of *flow states*, where an individual feels one with everything that is arising in any state. Call that **nondual mysticism**.

Now, the point is that you can have any of these spiritual state experiences at virtually any stage of development, simply because at every stage you happen to wake, dream, and sleep. You can be at, say, orange altitude in any of the developmental lines and have a gross, subtle, causal, or nondual peak experience.

One of the things that researchers have learned over the past three decades about the relationship between states and stages is extraordinarily important: you will interpret any spiritual (meditative, altered) *state* of consciousness according to your *stage* of consciousness. That is, according to your *altitude* of development. (Actually, of course, one will interpret one's experience according to one's entire AQAL matrix, but levels/stages are a particularly important component of that overall interpretation, and the one we are emphasizing here.)

To give an example of this, let's use a simple 7-level scheme of *stages of consciousness* (archaic, magic, mythic, rational, pluralistic, integral, super-integral) and 4 types of *states of consciousness* (gross, subtle, causal, nondual), which gives us 4×7 or 28 types of spiritual or religious experience. And we have found evidence for every single one of them. . . .

This grid or lattice of state/stage combinations is called the **Wilber-Combs Lattice**, after its two founders (and after months of my explaining to Allan Combs how silly "The Combs-Wilber Lattice" sounded). Figure 17 gives one example of the W-C Lattice.

Let me give a quick example of how this Lattice works. Let's say a person has a peak experience of seeing a cloud of radiant white luminosity, which at times appears to be a person or being of light, and then has a sense of merging into that light, feeling a sense of infinite love and unbounded bliss. Let's say that this person is a Protestant, whose Lower-Left

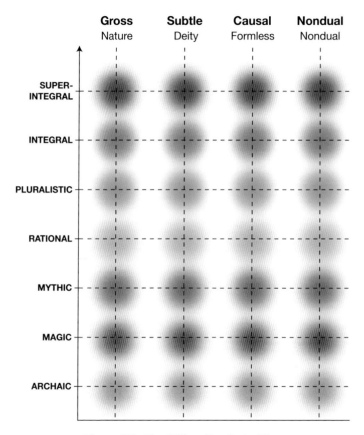

Figure 17. *The Wilber-Combs Lattice.*

quadrant has predisposed his interpretations to see and clothe this experience in Christian terms. What will this person see?

If he's at **red** altitude, he might see this as a magical Jesus who can walk on water, resurrect the dead, turn water into wine, multiply loaves and fishes, and so on. At **amber**, he might see Jesus as the eternal lawgiver, the bringer of complete salvation if one believes the myths and dogmas and follows the codes, commandments, and covenants given to the chosen people and found in the one and only true Book (the Bible). At **orange**, this person might see Jesus as a universal humanist, yet also divine, teaching worldcentric love and morality, and who can bring salvation not just in heaven but to some degree on this earth, in this life. At **green**, this person might see Jesus as one of many, equally valid spiritual teachers, and hence embracing Jesus might give complete salvation for me, which is why I passionately do so, but other individuals and cultures might find other spiritual paths to be better for them, knowing that all genuine spiritual paths, if they go deep enough, can offer an equal salvation or liberation. If this person is flying at **turquoise**, he might see Jesus as a manifestation of the same Christ-consciousness that everybody, including you and me, can have complete access to, and thus Jesus is emblematic of a transformative consciousness that shows each person to be part of a vast system of dynamic, flowing, and mutually interpenetrating processes that includes all of us in its radiant sweep. At **violet** and **ultraviolet**, Christ-consciousness might be seen as emblematic of the transcendental, infinite, selfless Self, the divine consciousness that was in Jesus and is in you and in me, a radically all-inclusive consciousness of Light, Love, and Life that is resurrected from the stream of time upon the death of the loveless and self-contracting ego, revealing a destiny beyond death, beyond suffering, beyond space and time and tears and terror, and hence found to be right here, right now, in the timeless moment in which all reality comes to be.

In other words, the altered-state experience will be interpreted, in part, according to the stage that one is at. There is a magic Christ, a mythic Christ, a rational Christ, a pluralistic Christ, an integral and super-integral Christ, and so on. This, of course, is true of any experience, but it becomes particularly important with spiritual and religious experiences. A person can be at a fairly low-level stage of development, such as red or amber, and yet have a fully authentic subtle- or causal-state experience.

The reborn fundamentalist and evangelical is a very common example. This person *knows* that they have experienced Christ (or Allah, or Mary, or Brahman) personally, and nothing you can say will even begin to convince them otherwise. And it's half true: they have had an authentic, vivid, real, and immediate experience of a subtle-state reality. But they are interpreting that state through stages that are egocentric or ethnocentric: Jesus, and only Jesus, has the

one true way. Worse, their real or authentic state experience of love will actually *reinforce* their ethnocentrism. Only those who accept Jesus as their personal savior can find salvation; everybody else is consigned to eternal damnation and hellfire by an all-loving and all-forgiving God. Does that intense contradiction make any sense? Well, it does if you use the W-C Lattice.

The existence of states of consciousness allows us to see why people can have experiences that are very spiritual and very authentic, in some ways, even if they are at relatively low levels of development. This is also why they can be so commonplace. While the percentage of the population that is at the very highest (third-tier) levels of development in any of the lines appears to be less than 1%, those who report having had some sort of spiritual or religious experience is well over 75%, according to many polls. Using IOS, all of this otherwise completely conflicting data begins to make sense: 1% have had *higher-stage* spiritual experiences; 75% have had *altered-state* spiritual experiences.

Of course, the ideal situation for a person is to be at the higher stages of development as well as have a broad range of significant state experiences, such as meditative and contemplative states. As it is now, some spiritual practitioners focus only on meditative states, unaware or disdainful of developmental stages, which is unfortunate. Combining both is one of the main aims of an Integral Life Practice, which we will return to in the next chapter.

Quadrants: Where Is Ultimate Reality?

We have seen that what people are referring to as "spirituality" can be something that is occurring in the highest levels or stages of any line, or it can be a developmental line itself, or it can refer to various altered states of consciousness: levels, lines, and states. What about types and quadrants?

We can do this part very quickly, since the basic idea is now apparent, I think. "Types" is an important aspect or definition of spirituality, in that many people equate "spiritual" with some type of quality, such as love, kindness, equanimity, wisdom, and so on.

While this is true, if you look at each of those qualities, it becomes obvious that they show development. We saw this with Carol Gilligan and the quality of care or compassion, which develops from selfish to care to universal care to integrated. So although we definitely include types, it usually reverts very quickly to one of the previous definitions involving levels and/or lines. For example, we might say that spirituality involves love, and that to be spiritual is to be loving. But love itself develops from egocentric love to ethnocentric love to worldcentric love to Kosmocentric love, and only the higher of those levels are truly spiritual. Narcissistic or egocentric love is not usually thought of as terribly spiritual. So those who say, "All we need is love," haven't fully thought through their position very well.

Quadrants come into play when various theorists are trying to explain what they think is the "really real" makeup of the world (fig. 18). Where is ultimate reality in your conception? Not just what level is your God, but what quadrant is your God?

Is matter the primary reality? Or are spirit and consciousness the primary ingredients? Or perhaps you think that all of

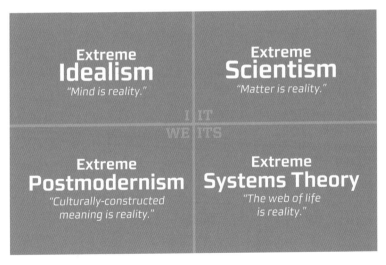

Figure 18. *Quadrant Absolutism.*

those "superstructures" of religion can be reduced to the "base" of economic realities? Or perhaps that all our knowledge is just a social construction?

If you think matter is the ultimate reality (i.e., the Upper-Right quadrant is the only real quadrant), then any spiritual experience or belief will be nothing but an illusion, an epiphenomena of brain states and their physiological fireworks. God is just an imaginary friend for grown-ups. All such spiritual beliefs are "nothing but" physical fireworks in the material brain.

If you think spirit and consciousness (Upper-Left quadrant) are the ultimate realities, then you will believe just the opposite: the entire world of material form is the fallen realm of illusion, and those who believe in it are lost in ignorance, sin, maya, samsara.

If you think the systems view of reality (the Lower-Right quadrant) is the ultimate view, then all religious and spiritual beliefs are nothing but manifest structure-functions that are determined by the "real" realities of social system, the techno-economic base, and interwoven webs of dynamic processes, all as 3rd-person *its* and nothing but 3rd-person *its*.

And if you think the Lower-Left quadrant is the only real quadrant, then all aspects of knowledge—including all of our ideas about systems themselves, not to mention God and Spirit—are nothing but *social constructions*. Not "I" nor "it" nor "its" are finally real, but rather the almighty "we" creates literally all reality.

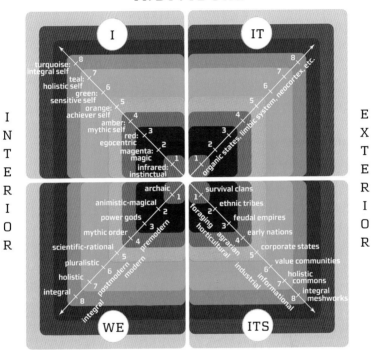

Figure 19. *AQAL.*

Doesn't this kind of **quadrant absolutism** bore the daylights out of you? It does me, I must confess. For AQAL, all of the quadrants are equi-primordial; none are more real or primary than the others; they all tetra-arise and tetra-evolve together. Ultimate reality, if it is to be found anywhere, is found in their simultaneous arising and radiant display, mutually creating and mutually sustaining each other.

Is Spirit Real or Not?

With all of this research on higher states and stages of awareness, can we finally say with any sort of confidence whether there is or is not a real Spirit, a real Godhead, a real Ground of All Being?

I'll repeat that if we are going to try to decide that ultimate question, it would certainly help if we checked with the answers given by those at the highest stages of development, don't you think? Not that we have to believe everything they say, but simply check on whether they give some sort of consistent response here.

As you might expect, they do. And it is as previously suggested, namely, the ultimate Ground of Being is not pictured in magic terms or mythic terms, nor is it seen as something outside of or merely transcendent to this world, but rather the

Suchness or Thusness of this world, or even the Emptiness of all that is arising (with "Emptiness" meaning the unqualifiable openness or transparency of each moment). Sometimes it is described in terms that imply an ultimate Intelligence or present Awareness or infinite Consciousness. We are not talking about a mythic, dualistic intelligence that designs things deliberately the way a watchmaker creates watches. It is an intelligence that knows a thing by *being* it and simultaneously bringing it forth. It is the Self of all that exists, so that knowing and being, or subject and object, are one in a nondual presence. If it is described as a subject, it is a subject so free of objects that no descriptions whatsoever can capture it—a vast, open Witness, an Absolute Subjectivity, a Mirror Mind, which is one with its reflections and reflects them all impartially, equally, effortlessly, spontaneously, a Big Mind that endlessly embraces all, yet is fully here and now. If it is described in terms of Being, is it not an ontological substance but the Suchness or Is-ness of things, prior to concepts and feelings and thoughts and images, but easily touched right here and now as the simple feeling of Being. If it is described in personal terms, it is a Godhead beyond any God and Goddess, an Intelligence-Abyss from which all things issue in this moment. It is "eternal," not as something that is everlasting, but something that is ever-present, since the timeless Now is without time. (Didn't even Wittgenstein—the influential modern philosopher known for his insistence on facts and logic—say: "If we take eternity to mean not infinite temporal duration but timelessness, then eternal life belongs to those who live in the present"?) In other words, not something that goes on in time forever but a moment without time at all. An endless moment, it turns out, a timeless Now and pure Present that holds all time in the palm of its hand, if you but know where to find it.

There are as many "descriptions" of this Spirit as there are those at the ultraviolet waves of consciousness unfolding. Yet they all agree that Spirit—by whatever name and beyond all multiculturalism—is the Ground and Goal of all existence, an infinite Reality existing behind, beyond, above, within, and *as* the entire manifest universe.*

---

* Let's clarify a point for advanced students. What's the difference between, let's say, the overmind structure and the causal state, since they sound similar? Both have access to the Witness, but the overmind is a stage in structural development—and all development is envelopment, or a series of whole/parts or holons that transcend and include all previous development, and thus stages are inclusionary; whereas states are not inclusionary but exclusionary (e.g., you cannot be drunk and sober at the same time, nor awake and dreaming at the same time, nor in dreamless sleep and dreaming at the same time, etc.). Thus, the overmind structure-stage is a pure witnessing awareness that is also a unitive knowledge and awareness that includes all previous objects as they continue to arise (not excludes them); the overmind is thus a capacity to be aware of all previous structures, a 7th chakra that operates on the previous 6 chakras (which are now all fully present and conscious as "operands"). The causal state is a consciousness without objects, the same witnessing awareness but with nothing as its "object," a vast openness that is its own blissful operand. The former is an inclusive structure; the latter, an exclusive state. Even Buddhas continue to wake, dream, and sleep, which shows that even in Buddhas, states continue to be exclusionary in themselves, even though the Witness is now free of all of them and thus, in the overmind, all of their capacities can be and are integrated.

Is there a proof for that God? Yes, absolutely, and here it is: develop to the ultraviolet waves of your own awareness and then *look*. And taste, touch, feel, breathe, and tell us what you see.

But one thing is for sure: it is not a mythic God, it is not scientific materialism, it is not pluralism. All three of those have failed to give satisfactory answers to the riddle of existence, and that is exactly why. They were not yet whole enough to see the Big Picture of your own Being, your own Becoming, and your own Awakening.

Conclusion

The many faces of Spirit, indeed. . . .

Using the AQAL matrix, we realize that "spirituality" can be used, and has been used, to refer to quadrants, levels/stages, lines, states, and types. Each of these usages is valid, but we must state which aspect of spirituality we are referring to, because otherwise our conclusions are all diametrically opposed to each other and end up deeply contradictory. No wonder the field of spirituality remains perhaps the single most confused topic that any human can discuss.

But begin using IOS, and suddenly it all starts to make sense, at least enough to climb out of the nightmare of fun-

damentalism (amber), the depressing emptiness of scientific modernity (orange), or the wasteland of whatever (green). Moving in the direction of the supramental, transpersonal, and superconscious waves of evolution, Spirit itself seems to smile, announce its presence, and awaken to the umpteenth game of "hide and seek" with its own being and becoming.

There is a Spirit for each and every wave of awareness, since Spirit *is* that very Awareness appearing in the different levels of its own development, the same Awareness that slumbers in the mineral, stirs in the plant, moves in the animal, revives in the human, and returns to itself in the awakened sage. Most extraordinarily, all of us—including me and you—are invited to become an awakened sage ourselves.

Shall we see?

6

INTEGRAL LIFE PRACTICE: GET A LIFE!

The **purpose**

of an INTEGRAL LIFE PRACTICE

the FULL S P E C T of your

is to realize

R U M

UNIQUE
and *SPECIAL*
capacities

Through **DAILY PRACTICE** in a variety of AREAS or MODULES, you can experience greater

FREEDOM and **fullness** in your life

The awakened Sage is not merely a rare oddity, living alone in a cave in India or perched on a mountain top in Tibet. The awakened Sage—or simply awakened Human—is actually the nature of our very own consciousness, even here and now, in the deepest forms and highest waves. Realizing that is the goal of Integral Life Practice.

MOST OF THE "IOS APPS" WE HAVE LOOKED AT TEND TO FOCUS on some of the practical applications of the Integral Approach, in medicine, business, and ecology, and its use in helping to make sense of spirituality. What about the *experiential* and *practical* aspects of my own awareness, growth, transformation, and awakening?

The practical, 1st-person, experiential dimension of the Integral Approach is called **Integral Life Practice**, or **ILP**.

The basic nature of ILP is simple. If you take body, mind, and spirit (as levels), and self, culture, and nature (as quadrants), and then you combine them, you get 9 possible areas of growth and awakening. Integral Life Practice is the first approach to cross-combine all of those for the most effective personal transformation possible.

To give a slightly more expanded example: if you look at figure 8 (p. 76), you will notice that 3 levels in 4 quadrants gives you 12 zones. Integral Life Practice has created practical exercises for growth in all 12 zones, a radically unique and historically unprecedented approach to growth, development, and awakening.

Let's focus on the Upper quadrants—the individual quadrants—to see what is involved. These zones are so important that we refer to them as *the core modules*—body, mind, spirit, and shadow. To give an example of what is involved, I will give the "1-Minute Modules" that have been developed for each of them. These are considerably shortened versions of the extended modules, but these brief versions manage to capture the essentials of each module in a very condensed and distilled fashion. Of course, we recommend that you do the fuller versions of the various modules and practices, but the 1-Minute Modules are remarkably effective if you only have a short amount of time, or if you want to capture the flavor and some of the effects of the fuller versions.

Let me emphasize that you do not have to do the ILP version of an integral practice. You can create your own integral practice and have it be very effective. Simply use the general guidelines in this chapter and as summarized in the ILP Matrix (pp. 170–171). As you can see in that table, any number of practices can be used in the various modules. The idea is simply to pick one practice from the each of the basic modules and then engage them concurrently. You can add auxiliary modules if you wish, and then go! If you want to use the ILP Starter Kit designed by Integral Institute—or the *Integral Life Practice Handbook* (forthcoming from Integral Books)—that's fine, too, since the researchers at I-I have done most of the work for you and created in-depth instructional materials which considerably expand upon those given here (www.MyILP.com). But believe me, either way is just fine.

The Core Modules

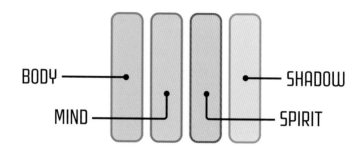

BODY ——————● SHADOW

MIND ——————● SPIRIT

Body, Mind, Spirit, and Shadow—these are the **core modules**. But if you think that this is the standard "New Age" or "holistic" or "spiritual" approach, that would be your first mistake.

Body Module

To begin with, "body" doesn't mean merely the typical feeling body of New-Age spirituality, nor is it the standard physical body of Western medicine. It's both of them, plus more. It refers to the gross physical body, the subtle energy body, and the causal transcendent body. ILP involves exercising all of them, or what we call **the 3-Body Workout**.

The 3-Body Workout includes exercises for the physical body, such as weightlifting and aerobics. It also incorporates exercises for the subtle body of emotion, imagination, and felt meaning, including variations on tai chi and qigong. And it includes exercises for the causal body, such as feeling to infinity and the circle of light and life.

Here are some of the 1-Minute Modules for the 3-Body Workout.

1-Minute Module
Strength Workout

This is a simplified form of any basic weightlifting exercise. It is the shortest and easiest way to keep muscles toned and strong. In this exercise, we strengthen our muscles by quickly challenging them to failure and then letting them recover. Our body regrows the muscle tissue in order to meet the same challenge the next time. By taking this principle of challenge, failure, and recovery into account, workouts can be extremely simple, quick, and effective.

To increase muscle strength, choose one muscle group to work on (e.g., biceps, chest, abs, legs). You

The Integral Life Practice™ Matrix

— CORE MODULES —

SAMPLE PRACTICES

Body (Physical, Subtle, Causal)	**Mind** (Framework, View)	**Spirit** (Meditation, Prayer)	**Shadow** (Therapia)
Weightlifting (Physical)	Reading & Study	Zen	Gestalt Therapy
Aerobics (Physical)	Belief System	Centering Prayer	Cognitive Therapy
F.I.T. ☆ (Physical, Subtle)	Integral (AQAL) Framework ☆	Big Mind ☆ Meditation	3-2-1 Process ☆
Diet: Atkins, Ornish, the Zone (Physical)	Mental Training	Kabbalah	Dream-Work
ILP Diet (Physical) ☆	Taking Multiple Perspectives	Compassionate Exchange ☆	Interpersonal
Tai Chi Chuan (Subtle)	Any Worldview or Meaning System that Works for You	TM	Psychoanalysis
Qi Gong (Subtle)		Integral Inquiry ☆	Art & Music Therapy
Yoga (Physical, Subtle)		Vipassana Meditation	
3-Body Workout (Physical, Subtle, Causal) ☆		The 1-2-3 of Spirit ☆	

AUXILIARY MODULES

Ethics	Sex	Work	Emotions	Relationships
Codes of Conduct	Tantra	Right Livelihood	Transmuting ⭐ Emotions	Integral ⭐ Relationships
Professional Ethics	Integral Sexual Yoga ⭐	Professional Training	Emotional Intelligence Training	Integral ⭐ Parenting
Social & Ecological Activism	Kama Sutra	Money Management	Bhakti Yoga (Devotional Practices)	Communication Skills
Self-Discipline	Kundalini Yoga	Work as a Mode of ILP ⭐	Emotional Mindfulness Practice	Couples Therapy
Integral Ethics ⭐	Sexual Transformative Practice	Karma Yoga	Tonglen (Compassionate Exchange Meditation)	Relational Spiritual Practice
Sportsmanship		Community Service & Volunteering		Right Association (Sangha)
Vows & Oaths		Work as Transformation	Creative Expression & Art	Conscious Marriage

It's as simple as:

- Pick **one practice** from each of the **Four Core Modules**
- Add practices from the **Auxiliary Modules** as you wish
- Go!

(We particularly recommend the Gold Star Practices ⭐)

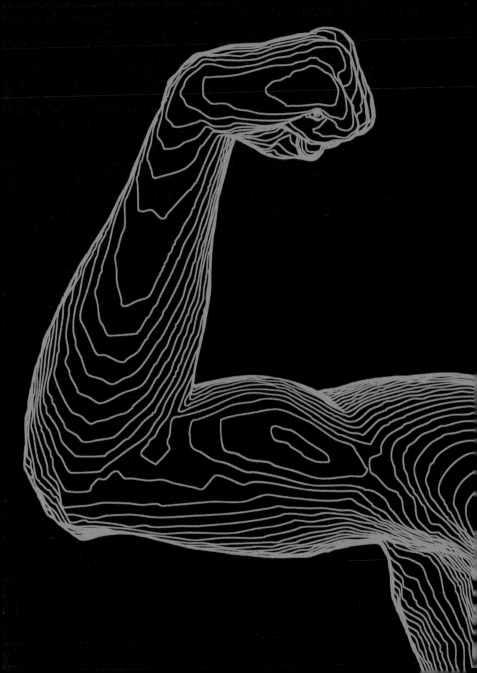

can use a barbell, dumbbells, a machine, or your own body weight (e.g., squats, push-ups, sit-ups). Warm up. Then do the exercise until you bring the muscle group to full exhaustion. If you're using weights, this should take somewhere between 8 to 12 repetitions. That's it—you're done!

One day, one set, one muscle group. For your next strength training session, simply choose a different muscle group . . . and repeat. A minute or two each day. You'll be shocked at the improvement in just one month. Try it!

1-Minute Module
Aerobic Workout

Research shows that increasing your aerobic capacity does not necessarily require extended runs or conditioning exercises. You can derive incredible benefits just with a few quick cycles of getting your heart rate up and then resting—also called *interval training*.

To improve cardiovascular health, pick any aerobic exercise that will raise your heart rate—it could be running, biking, or even jump-roping. Warm up, and then perform the activity until your heart-rate rises to about 80% of its maximum (about just when you start to get short of breath). Once there, stop the activity and completely rest for a brief period. Repeat 2 or 3 times.

NOTE: Due to the risk of injury, we recommend that beginners seek experienced guidance before performing this exercise.

1-MINUTE MODULE
3-BODY WORKOUT

1. Causal Body

Standing and breathing naturally . . .

Notice the suchness, the is-ness of this and every moment. I am this suchness. I am the openness in which all things arise.

Inhale, exhale, and inhale. Palms together at heart and then hands crossed over chest, and then, on last exhale, opening up both hands along either side . . .

I breathe out and release to infinity.

2. Subtle Body

Inhaling, hands gather energy, coming to fingers loosely interlaced . . .

I breathe into the fullness of life.

Exhaling, hands move up the front, palms facing the sky . . .

I breathe out and return to light.

Inhaling, hands come down along the sides, returning to fingers loosely interlaced . . .

Completing the circle, I am free and full.

Continue for a total of 8 arm circles, tongue on palate (completing the "microcosmic orbit"). Exhaling, hands move up the front to the sky; inhaling, hands circles back out and down.

3. Physical Body

Touch belly with hands, inhaling and exhaling . . .

Infinite freedom and fullness appear as this precious human body.

Inhaling and exhaling, squat gently, touching the ground . . .

Touching the earth, I am connected to all beings.

4. Dedication

Bow in Four Directions (turning right, clockwise).

May my consciousness / and my behavior / be of service to all beings / in all worlds / liberating all / into the suchness / of this and every moment.

Mind Module: The AQAL Framework

The module that is perhaps the most important in all of Integral Life Practice is the Mind module, simply because it is the missing link between body and spirit. Spiritual practitioners around the world commonly say that we need to include and honor "body, mind, and spirit," but, in fact, during the past two decades, mind has been left out of the equation almost entirely, and the feelings of the body have taken center stage, so much so that immediate feelings and experiences have often been equated with spiritual awareness itself. Mind or intellect has not only been left out, it has been called "non-spiritual" and even "anti-spiritual," the idea apparently being that you should "come from your heart," bypassing the obstruction known as your brain. "Don't intellectualize, don't conceptualize, but instead just feel, just be experiential"— those words rang out across the country as spiritual practitioners everywhere believed that, in order to find spirit, you must "lose your mind and come to your senses."

Well, try it. And after a decade or so of you losing your mind, you might decide to turn in the other direction. Mind is actually the link between body and spirit. Mind or intellect, in Sanskrit, is *buddhi*, from which all *Buddhas* are born. Mind is what holds body and spirit together. Mind issues straight from spirit, and is both the first expression of spirit and the highest level on the return to spirit. As the dimension between body and spirit, mind anchors spirit in the body and raises the body up to spirit, giving spirit its groundings, and giving the body its spiritual direction, which otherwise would be lost in its own sensations, sights, and sentiments. Spiritual growth itself moves from egocentric bodily feelings, which can only feel themselves, to mind, which can take the role of others and thus begin to expand beyond the ego, and from there into the worldcentric embrace of spirit. *To put yourself in somebody else's shoes* is a mental operation, a cognitive operation, and thus to feel feelings *other than your own* requires the mind, the intellect. It is mind that allows awareness to rise above the prison of its egocentric feelings and begin to radically expand beyond itself on the way to embracing the entire Kosmos—of feelings and thoughts and luminous awareness: body and mind and spirit, with mind the missing link.

Without a cohesive and comprehensive mental framework, things fall apart faster than you can sing "Feelings." Over the past three decades, one fact has surfaced time and time again: without a mental framework to actually hold spiritual experiences, those experiences just don't stick.

In Integral Life Practice, we use the AQAL View or Framework, simply because it is the only genuinely integral view that we are aware of at this time. AQAL is not a "mere

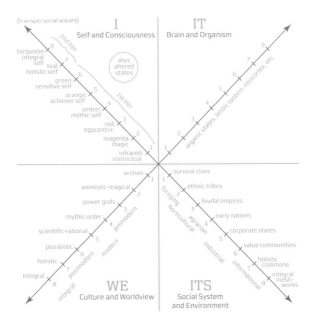

Figure 20. *The Four Quadrants in Humans.*

abstraction" but a living, luminous, experiential reality. In fact, most people report that it is **psychoactive**. Once you learn AQAL—or once you download IOS into your biocomputer—then it acts as an internal checklist, automatically alerting you to areas of your own capacities that you might not be utilizing as fully as you could. It imposes nothing from the outside, but lights up the insides of your own possibilities. It is also psychoactive in the sense of changing the very nature of what you thought was available in your own being. And, finally, it is fun: if you actually get it, it's not hard, it's thrilling.

Making Sense of Everything

Many people use a simple phrase to explain the excitement of working with the AQAL module—"Making sense of everything"—which is what the AQAL Framework helps to do. In fact, it was first designed as a way to index all of the various types of human activity. The result of over 30 years of research by myself and many other scholars, it delivered a way for us to classify and index all the major forms of knowledge and experience. (We used it that way in this book when we indexed the various meanings of "spirituality," for example.)

But it soon became obvious that it was useful in many other areas, including as a rather extraordinary map of our own awareness (or otherwise it wouldn't work as an indexing system). We then compared it with over 100 maps of the human bodymind from around the world—premodern, modern, and postmodern—and used all of them to fill in the gaps left by the others. That "composite map" had 5 simple elements, and that's how AQAL was born.

If you start using AQAL, you can check for yourself and

see if it starts to help you "make sense of everything." Take, for example, the conflict between religion and science. Barbara Walters recently had a TV special called "Heaven." In it, she first interviewed many of the most popular of today's spiritual teachers, such as the Dalai Lama, and each of them explained how deeply meaningful and significant spiritual life is to them. Then, in the second half of the show, she interviewed well-known scientists, every one of whom explained, in so many words, that spiritual experiences are nothing but physical fireworks in the material brain. There is no spirit, only matter, they explained, and people who believe in the former are obviously hooked on infantile illusions and whatnot.

It was so weird watching this, because you soon realize that the way everybody on this show was thinking, if either half of them is right, the other half is dead wrong. If the scientists are right, the spiritual authorities are all caught in illusions—*and vice versa!* Either way, half of all humans are spending their lives on nothing but illusions! It makes no sense at all.

What does make sense is that they are both right. The spiritual folks are talking about the Upper-Left quadrant, and the scientists are talking about the Upper-Right quadrant.

Or take the **culture wars**. If the above example relates particularly to quadrants, the culture wars relate especially to levels. Although there are many different aspects to the culture wars, they focus on an intense battle between **traditional** values, **modern** values, and **postmodern** values.

These are almost exactly *amber*, *orange*, and *green* altitudes, respectively. Remember that all first-tier levels believe that their values are the only real values anywhere in existence, with all the others caught in deep confusion at best, total illusion at worst. Well, welcome to the culture wars! It's literally almost that simple.

What we are awaiting, of course, is the great leap to second tier, where the first genuine integration of the various levels starts to take place, and where one's awareness rises above the crossfire of the culture wars and into the spacious openness of integral awareness, on the way to its own suprapersonal realization and enlightenment. In this and so many other areas, using an Integral or AQAL Framework,

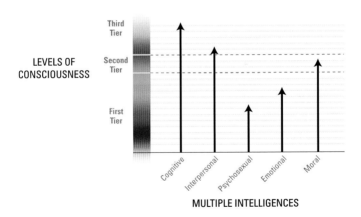

Figure 21. *Levels and Lines.*

suddenly things make sense. Suddenly there is a place for everything in your life. A great depth of peace and certainty descends on your being, as the mind makes room for all of the Kosmos, and not just a little simpering slice of it here and there. Joy returns to thought; the intellect actually lights up—and lightens up—as it's supposed to; and luminous clarity defines each moment in the world of all things integral.

Most importantly, there is indeed a place for everything in your life. Everything has meaning, because everything fits. *Meaning* returns to one's life. This is perhaps the single most important and quickly noticeable item about the Integral Approach: everything fits, and thus meaning returns.

On the other side of irony, there is meaning. On the other side of a fractured and fragmented world, there is meaning. On the other side of despair, there is meaning. Try the Integral Framework out for just a while, give it a test drive, and see what you think. But whatever framework or view you use, please make it as large and encompassing as you can, because the meaningfulness of your life almost certainly depends on it.

Here is the 1-Minute Module for the Mind, or Integral (AQAL) Framework, focusing on three levels (body, mind, spirit) and four quadrants (the "big three" of I, we, and it). It's called "Get a Feel for AQAL," because this Framework is not a mere abstraction but a map of a felt and living reality.

1-MINUTE MODULE
GET A FEEL FOR AQAL

The cornerstone of the AQAL Framework is an understanding of *perspectives*. In any moment, you can feel these basic dimensions of your being, simply by noticing what is already present.

- *Feel your present I-space or individual awareness. What does it feel like to be an "I" right now?* **Feel** *that I-ness.*

- *Feel your present We-space or intersubjective awareness. What does it feel like to be in relationship to others right now? (If no other people are present, you can imagine a significant other, your family, or your co-workers. You can even try to feel what connects you to someone on the other side of the world.)* **Feel** *that We-ness.*

- *Feel your present It-space or objective world. What is physically surrounding you? What does the ground feel like beneath your feet?* **Feel** *that It-ness.*

- *Now, feel your body—your feelings and sensations.*

- *Feel your mind—your thoughts and images.*

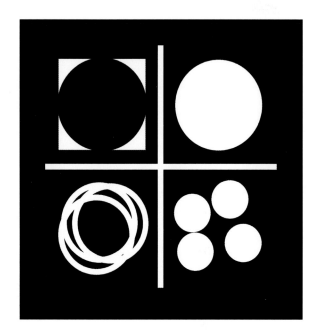

- *Finally, feel the witness or Spirit of this and every moment—that which is aware of your I, we, it, body, and mind, right now.*

- *Silently remind yourself, "These are all dimensions of my being and becoming, all of which I will include, none of which I will reject."*

You have just felt a very brief version of AQAL—all quadrants (I, We, It), and all levels (Body, Mind, and

Spirit). This is exercising **body, mind,** and **spirit** in **self, culture,** and **nature.**

Shadow Module

If I said I thought the Mind module was the most important module, I've changed my mind: the Shadow module is. (Well, they're all important, yes?) Another one of the lessons that we learned the very hard way over the last few decades is that if you don't do shadow work, virtually every other module can get sabotaged, and worst of all, by your own unconscious motives.

The "shadow" is a term representing the personal unconscious, or the psychological material that we repress, deny, dissociate, or disown. Unfortunately, denying this material doesn't make it go away; on the contrary, it returns to plague us with painful neurotic symptoms, obsessions, fears, and anxieties. Uncovering, befriending, and re-owning this material is necessary not only for removing the painful symptoms, but for forming an accurate and healthy self-image.

Take, for example, somebody who is uncomfortable with their own feelings of anger or aggression. Whenever placed in circumstances where the average person might get angry, or at least damned irritated, this individual won't feel his own

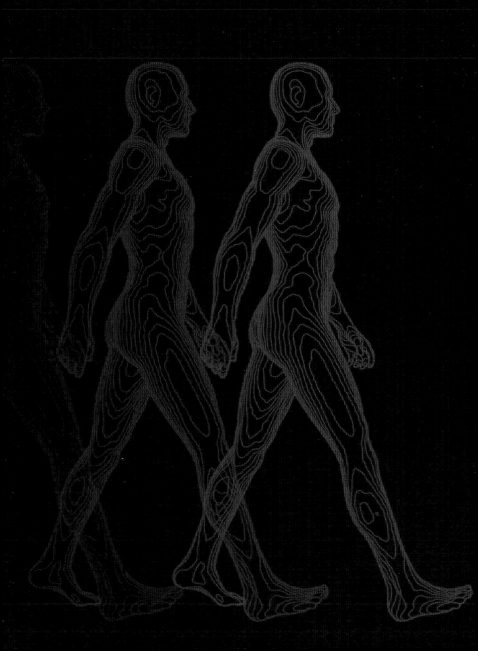

anger because he represses it. The anger doesn't thereby disappear, but is simply displaced or projected onto somebody else. Since he knows somebody is angry as hell, and since it can't possibly be him, it must be somebody else—anybody else. Come to think of it, his boss seems to be really angry at him! And this makes him incredibly depressed. His own feelings of anger have been repressed, alienated, and disowned, only to return as feelings of alienation and depression. M-A-D has become S-A-D, as this individual shadow-boxes his way through a rather unhappy life.

It used to be thought that meditation alone would uncover or "de-repress" most types of unconscious shadow material. But after several decades of people doing meditation, millions of shadows remained intact. The reasons for this were sought, and the bottom line seems to be that unless you know exactly what you are looking for, the panoramic awareness of meditation is too much of a shotgun approach to get at specific shadow elements. For this, laser psychotherapy is required.

In the above example, because meditation increases your capacity for sensitivity and feeling-awareness, then meditation might help this person get more in touch with his feelings of sadness and depression. He might be able to bring an enormous amount of awareness to flood the contours of his feelings of depression!—but this individual will not necessarily discover the anger and rage hidden and secreted in his feelings of depression unless he knows exactly where and how to look. This psychological detective work is the province of the great

depth psychologies, which was largely a discovery of the modern West. Meditation can help, but not replace, psychotherapy.

There are many effective forms of shadow psychotherapy, from Gestalt therapy to psychoanalytic therapy to Transactional Analysis. Other forms of psychotherapy, although

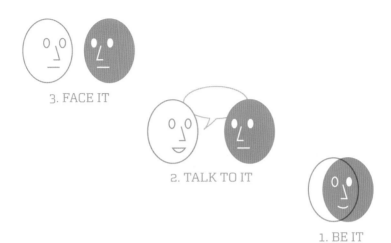

3. FACE IT

2. TALK TO IT

1. BE IT

they don't deal directly with the shadow, can also be very effective in correcting neurotic disorders. The helpfulness of cognitive and interpersonal approaches is particularly well documented. Even inner journaling and voice dialoguing can help. We refer to all of these as "shadow work."

But whichever form you may choose, no integral life practice is complete without some sort of shadow work. The simple suggestion is, don't learn this lesson the hard way, because your shadow can accompany you all the way to Enlightenment and back. The shadow is just one tricky little son of a bitch, which I suppose is how you get to be the shadow in the first place.

Here is the 1-Minute Shadow Module, which we call "The

3-2-1 of Shadow Work" because it helps take "it" symptoms and convert them to re-owned aspects of the self by **facing** the shadow as a 3rd person, **talking** to it as a 2nd person, then **being** it as a 1st person. FACE-TALK-BE.

1-MINUTE MODULE
3-2-1 PROCESS

You can do the 3-2-1 Process anytime you need it. Two particularly useful times are right when you wake up in the morning and just before going to bed at night. Once you know 3-2-1, it only takes a minute to do for anything that might be disturbing you.

First thing in the morning (before getting out of bed) review your dreams and find someone who showed up with an emotional charge, positive or negative. FACE that person, holding them in mind. Then TALK to that person, or simply resonate with them. Finally, BE that person by taking their perspective. For the sake of this exercise, there is no need to write anything out—you can go through the whole process right in your own mind.

Before going to bed, choose a person who either disturbed or attracted you during the day. FACE them, TALK to them, and then BE them (as described above).

Again, you can do the 3-2-1 process quietly by yourself, any time you need it, day or night.

Auxiliary (or Supplementary) Modules

The Body, Mind, Spirit, and Shadow modules are considered to be the **core** modules because: one, they are so essential; and two, they can be done by working on yourself, mostly.
The **auxiliary** modules are those that start to address your
relationships, your job or work in the world, your family, marriage life, and intimate partnerships—as well as advanced
aspects of individual work.

Foremost among these is the **Ethics Module**. In a recent
Integral Institute poll, which was sent out to some 8,000 members of www.IntegralNaked.org, an online radio program, we
asked those taking the poll, "What modules would you most
like to include in your own Integral Life Practice?" Choices included items such as meditation, work, relationships, diet,
and sexuality. The #1 choice was meditation; the #2 choice
was ethics. Over food, relationships, and sex, people chose
ethics. Apparently our culture is so bereft of moral compass,
individuals are absolutely starved for some sort of guidance
in this area.

The Ethics Module focuses on two basic orienting generalizations. The first is that *an action is moral or ethical the more perspectives it takes into account*. Actions that take only a 1st-person perspective into account are **egocentric**. Actions that take a 2nd-person perspective into account are **ethnocentric**. Actions that take a 3rd-person perspective into account are **worldcentric**. And actions that take a 4th- and 5th-person perspective are **Kosmocentric**.

Given that understanding, it's not hard to see, is it?, that worldcentric actions are *better* than ethnocentric actions. Worldcentric is *better* (or *more moral*) than ethnocentric, which is better than egocentric, because it takes more perspectives into account. As with Carol Gilligan's sequence (**selfish** to **care** to **universal care** to **integral**), each higher level is capable of being more ethical because it is capable of taking more perspectives into account before reaching a decision. Who would you want making decisions that affected you, somebody who is egocentric or somebody who is worldcentric?

So perhaps we can already see that there is a path that transcends the moral absolutism of amber and the moral relativism of green. With Integral Ethics, meaning returns, along with a moral compass that transcends and includes lesser perspectives.

The second orienting generalization is that ethical action is action that seeks to **protect and promote the greatest depth for the greatest span**. This maxim is known as the

Basic Moral Intuition, or BMI. *Depth* is defined as the number of levels in a holon, and *span* is the number of holons on a level. If we number the labeled levels in figure 14, then infrared has a (relative) depth of 1, red has 3, orange has 5, turquoise has 8, violet has 10, and so on.

But it is not enough to know that 8 is better than 5, which is better than 3. We also have to know how that fits in with other holons, human and nonhuman alike. A human has more depth than a cow, which has more depth than a carrot, which has more depth than a bacterium, which has more depth than a quark. So if we were forced to choose which to kill—a cow or a bacterium—we choose the bacterium. But because everything is interconnected, we don't act simply to promote more depth, but the most depth across the most span. Ecological awareness—and ecological ethics—involves this incredible balancing act between saving the most depth across the most span. Choosing just depth is anthropocentric; choosing just span is bacteria-centric. We act instead to protect and promote the greatest depth for the greatest span, or our Basic Moral Intuition.

Other auxiliary modules include Transmuting Emotions, Karma Yoga (or Work in the World), Sexual Yoga, Relationships, Family and Parenting. Please see www.integrallife.com for updates on these and other modules.

We now have one core module left to discuss, and I've changed my mind again. I think this is the most important module of all.

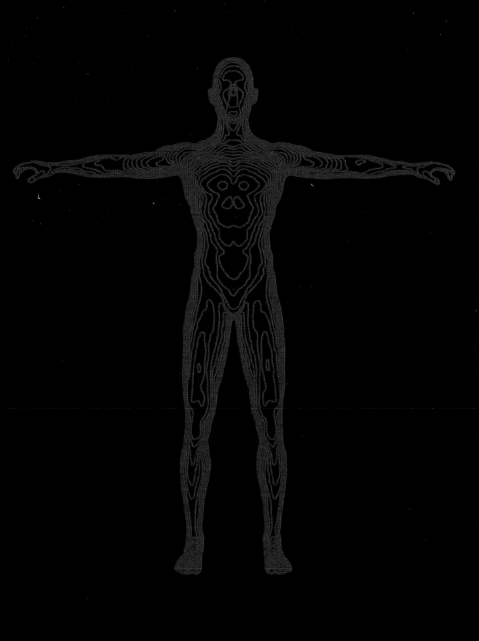

Spirit Module: The Vast Openness of Your Own Big Mind and Big Heart

We have seen that it's common nowadays for people to say that they are "spiritual but not religious." The general idea is that "religious" means institutional forms of religion—its dogma, myths, mandatory beliefs, its old and faded rituals; whereas "spiritual" means personal values, present awareness, interior realities, and immediate experience. Of course, some aspects of religion are spiritual, but much of institutional religion does indeed seem old and worn out, a relic of premodern times, or at least prerational stages of development.

Spirit can mean direct experience of a Ground of Being. It can mean anything that expresses one's ultimate concern. It can mean whatever gives life a sense of oneness or transcendence. It can mean one's own deepest nature and condition. We explored many of these in chapter 5. But the fact is, you either believe in a spiritual dimension of being or you don't. Because the core spiritual module focuses on the practice of meditation or contemplation, it is designed to accommodate the widest possible range of orientations, from the more "scientific" (meditation is a relaxation response) to the more "spiritual" (meditation gives access to an ultimate Ground of Being, or God by whatever name). Use whichever of those, or any others, that are comfortable for you.

A fairly unique feature of Integral Life Practice is what is called "The Three Faces of Spirit," or sometimes "The One-Two-Three (or 1-2-3) of God." The idea is that Spirit, as it manifests, has 4 quadrants, just like the rest of manifestation, and so, to the extent we think about Spirit, we can do so using the 4 quadrants (or simply the 1st-, 2nd-, and 3rd-person perspectives of Spirit).

Spirit in 3rd-person appears as a Great Web of Life, the entire Totality of Existence conceived as a Great It, a Great System of All Beings, or Nature with a capital *N*. Spinoza made this conception of God famous.

Spirit in 2nd-person is a Great You or Great Thou, a Living Intelligence and Love that is the ground and reason of all existence. The theistic traditions of the West especially focus on this face of Spirit.

Spirit in 1st-person is a Great I or I-I, the I that Witnesses the I, the pure infinite Self, the Atman that is Brahman, the Big Mind that is your real mind or awareness in this and every moment. The Eastern contemplative traditions especially focus on this face of Spirit.

Which of those faces is right? All of them, of course. They are the 4 quadrants—or three Faces—of manifest Spirit. You can use whichever of those perspectives feels right to you, but there is a special type of integral spiritual awareness that comes from using all of them, which is the approach we take.

Here is the 1-Minute Module for Spirit, focusing on all three faces.

1-MINUTE MODULE
THE 1-2-3 OF GOD

At any moment, you can experience God as a 3rd-person "It," a 2nd-person "Thou," or a 1st-person "I." Simply repeat the following sentences quietly to yourself, letting each perspective arise gently and naturally within your awareness.

- *I contemplate God as all that is arising—the Great Perfection of this and every moment.*

- *I behold and commune with God as an infinite Thou, who bestows all blessings and complete forgiveness on me, and before whom I offer infinite gratitude and devotion.*

- *I rest in God as my own Witness and primordial Self, the Big Mind that is one with all, and in this ever-present, easy, and natural state, I go on about my day.*

If you wish, you can replace the word "God" with any word of your choice that evokes an Ultimate Being. It could be "Spirit," "Jehovah," "Allah," "Brahman," "The Lord," or "The One."

Here is the same meditation with a more 1st-person orientation.

Notice your present awareness. Notice the objects arising in your awareness—the images and thoughts arising in your mind, the feelings and sensations arising in your body, the myriad objects arising around you in the room or environment. All of these are objects arising in your awareness.

Now think about what was in your awareness 5 minutes ago. Most of the thoughts have changed, most of the bodily sensations have changed, and probably most of the environment has changed. But something has not changed. Something in you is the same now as it was 5 minutes ago. What is present now that was present 5 minutes ago?

I AMness. The feeling-awareness of I AMness is still present. I am that ever-present I AMness. That I AMness is present now, it was present a moment ago, it was present a minute ago, it was present 5 minutes ago.

What was present 5 hours ago?

I AMness. That sense of I AMness is an ongoing, self-knowing, self-recognizing, self-validating I AMness. It is present now, it was present 5 hours ago. All my thoughts have changed, all my bodily sensations have changed, my environment has changed, but I AM is ever-present, radiant, open, empty, clear, spacious, transparent, free. Objects have changed, but not this formless I AMness. This obvious and present I AMness is present now as it was present 5 hours ago.

What was present 5 years ago?

I AMness. So many objects have come and gone, so many feelings have come and gone, so many thoughts have come and gone, so many dramas and terrors and loves and hates have come, and stayed awhile, and gone. But one thing has not come, and one thing has not gone. What is that? What is the only thing present in your awareness right now that you can remember was present 5 years ago? This timeless, ever-present feeling of I AMness is present now as it was 5 years ago.

What was present 5 centuries ago?

All that is ever-present is I AMness. Every person feels this same I AMness—because it is not a body, it is not a thought, it is not an object, it is not the environment, it is not anything that can be seen, but rather is the ever-present Seer, the ongoing open and empty Witness of all that is arising, in any person, in any world, in any place, at any time, in all the worlds until the end of time, there is only and always this obvious and immediate I AMness. What else could you possibly know? What else does anybody ever know? There is only and always this radiant, self-knowing, self-feeling, self-transcending I AM-ness, whether present now, 5 minutes ago, 5 hours ago, 5 centuries ago.

5 millennia ago?

Before Abraham was, I AM. Before the universe was, I AM. This is my original Face, the face I had before my parents were born, the face I had before the universe was born, the Face I had for all eternity until I decided to play this round of hide and seek, and get lost in the objects of my own creation.

I will NEVER again pretend that I do not know or feel my own I AMness.

And with that, the game is undone. A million thoughts have come and gone, a million feelings have come and gone, a million objects have come and gone. But one thing has not come, and one thing has not gone: the great Unborn and the great Undying, which never enters or leaves the stream of time, a pure Presence above time, floating in eternity. I am this great, obvious, self-knowing, self-validating, self-liberating I AMness.

Before Abraham was, I AM.

I AM is none other than Spirit in 1ˢᵗ-person, the ultimate, the sublime, the radiant all-creating Self of the entire Kosmos, present in me and you and him and her and them—as the I AMness that each and every one of us feels.

Because in all the known universes, the overall number of I AMs is but one.

Rest as I AMness always, the exact I AMness you feel right now, which is Unborn Spirit itself shining in and as you. Assume your personal identity as well—as this or that object, or this or that self, or this and that thing—resting always in the Ground of it All, as this great and completely obvious I AMness, and get up and go on about your day, in the universe I AM created.

chapter

7

NOT THE END, BUT THE BEGINNING

Look!

Look!

What do you see?

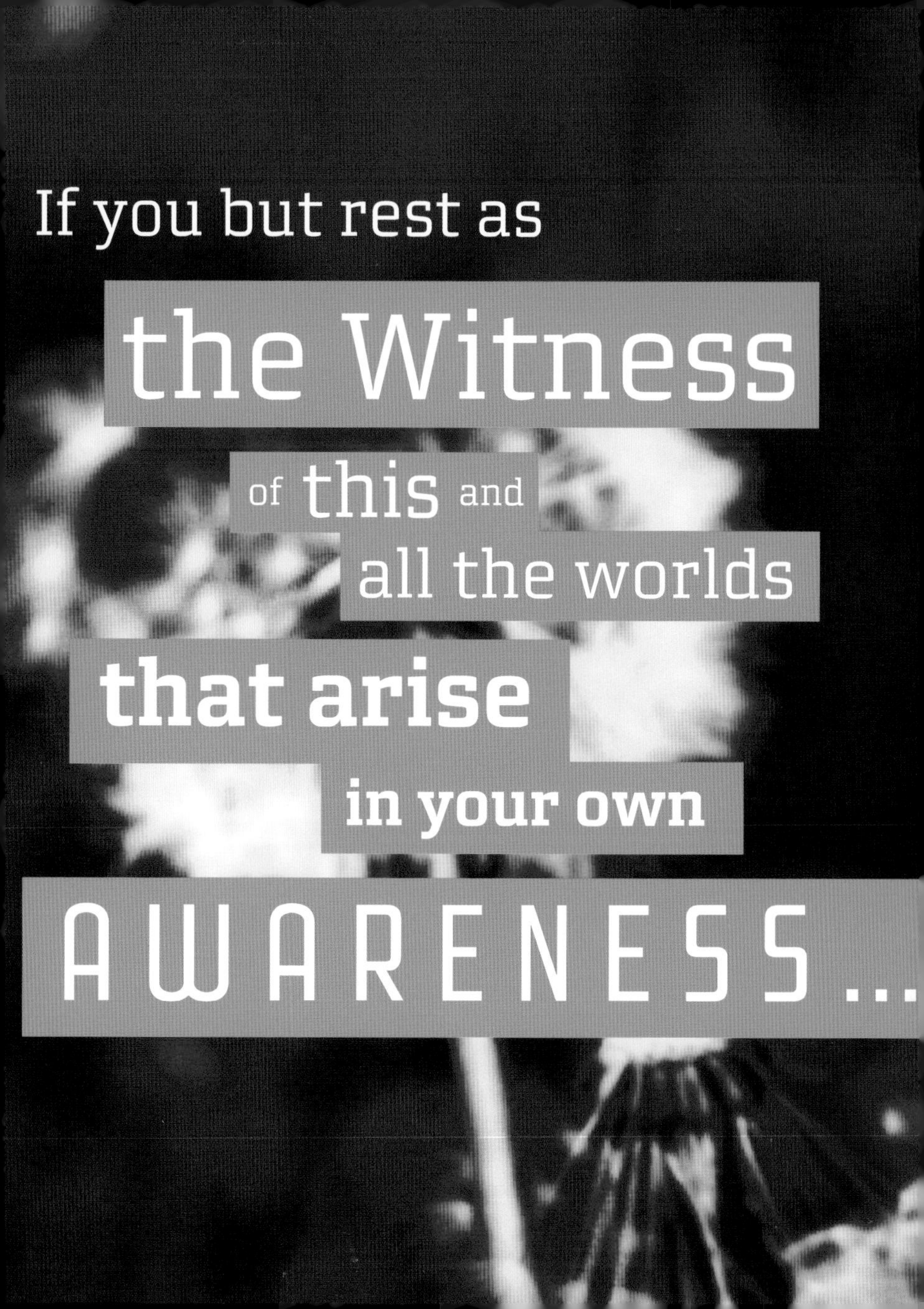

If you but rest as

the Witness

of this and
all the worlds

that arise

in your own

AWARENESS ...

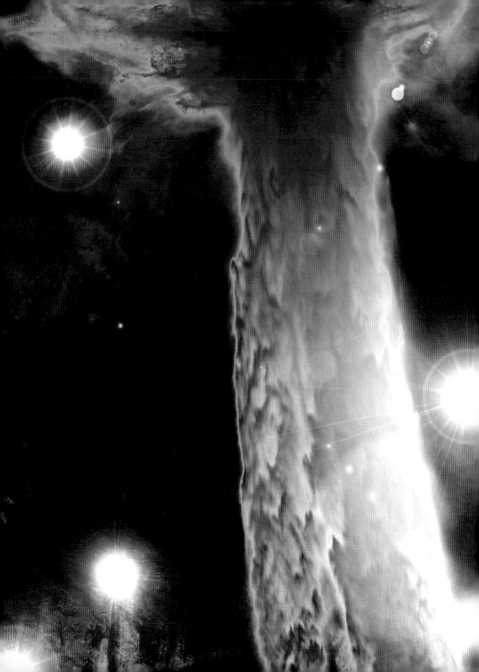

AQAL or **IOS** itself is just a map, nothing more. It is not the territory. But, as far as we can tell, it is the most comprehensive map that we possess at this time. Moreover—and this is important—the Integral Map itself insists that we go to the real territory and not get caught in mere words, ideas, or concepts. Remember that the quadrants are just a version of 1st-, 2nd-, and 3rd-person realities? Well, the **Integral Map** and **AQAL** and **IOS** are just 3rd-person words, they are abstractions, a series of "it" signs and symbols. But those 3rd-person words themselves insist that we also include 1st-person direct feelings, experiences, and consciousness as well as 2nd-person dialogue, contact, and interpersonal care. The Integral Map itself says: *this map is just a 3rd-person map, so don't forget those other important realities, all of which should be included in any comprehensive approach.*

WE'VE SEEN A FEW OF THE APPLICATIONS OR "APPS" OF THE Integral Model. We can now conclude with a brief summary of the main points of the model itself.

AQAL is short for "**all quadrants, all levels**"—which itself is short for "all quadrants, all levels, all lines, all states, all types," which are simply 5 of the most basic elements that need to be included in any truly integral or comprehensive approach.

When AQAL is used as a guiding framework to organize or understand any activity, we also call it an **Integral Operating System,** or simply **IOS**. More advanced forms of IOS are available, but **IOS Basic**, which this book introduced, has all of the essential elements (quadrants, levels, lines, states, types) to get anybody started toward a more comprehensive, inclusive, and effective approach.

When AQAL or IOS is used for real-life personal growth and development, we speak of **Integral Life Practice**, which appears to be the most comprehensive and therefore effective path of transformation available. The researchers at Integral Institute have attempted to create a simple, easy, introductory version of this, called the **ILP Starter Kit**, which you may be interested in checking out. I hate sales pitches, but I don't know any other way to get across the fact that an ILP Starter Kit is available, and at least a few people think it's pretty cool. Check it out: www.MyILP.com.

Here's one other important conclusion. IOS is a **neutral framework**; it does not tell you what to think, or force any particular ideologies on you, or coerce your awareness in any fashion. For example, to say that human beings have waking, dreaming, and deep sleep states is not to say what you should think while awake or what you should see while dreaming. It simply says, if you want to be comprehensive, be sure and include waking and dreaming and formless states.

Likewise, to say that all occasions have 4 quadrants—or simply "I," "we," and "it" dimensions—is not to say what the "I" should do, or the "we" should do, or the "it" should do. It simply says, if you are trying to include all the important possibilities, be sure to include 1st- and 2nd- and 3rd-person perspectives, because they are present in all major languages the world over.

Precisely because IOS is a neutral framework, it can be used to bring more clarity, care, and comprehensiveness to virtually any situation, making success much more likely, whether that success be measured in terms of personal transformation, social change, excellence in business, care for others, or simple happiness in life.

But perhaps most important of all, because IOS can be used by any discipline—from medicine to art to business to spirituality to politics to ecology—then we can, for the first time in history, begin an extensive and fruitful dialogue between all of these disciplines. A person using IOS in business can talk easily and effectively with a person using IOS in poetry, dance, or the arts, simply because they now have a common language—or a common operating system—with

which to communicate. When you are using IOS, not only can you run hundreds of different "software" programs on it, all of those programs can now communicate with each other and learn from each other, thus advancing an evolutionary unfolding to even greater dimensions of being and knowing and doing.

This is why thousands of scholars and teachers the world over came together and started Integral Institute, the world's first integral learning community. Because all of the various human activities, previously separated by incommensurate jargon and terminologies, can in fact begin to effectively communicate with each other by running an Integral Operating System, each of those disciplines can begin to converse with, and learn from, the others. This has never effectively happened anywhere in history, which is why, indeed, the Integral adventure is about to begin.

However we look at it, it all comes down to a few simple points. In your own growth and development, you have the capacity to take self, culture, and nature to increasingly higher, wider, and deeper modes of being, expanding from an isolated identity of "me" to a fuller identity of "us" to an even deeper identity with "all of us"—with all sentient beings everywhere—as your own capacity for Truth and Goodness and Beauty deepens and expands. Ever-greater consciousness with an ever-wider embrace, which is realized in self, embodied in nature, and expressed in culture.

Thus, **to cultivate body, mind, and spirit in self, culture,**

and nature. This is the extraordinary aim and goal of the Integral Approach, and we would love to have you join us in this exciting endeavor.

There is a new adventure here, and a new politics here, and even a new revolution, waiting on the horizon. You sense it, yes?

New work to be done, new glories to be told, new ground to be revealed, and secrets of the heart yet to unfold when it is too full to speak, too radiant to see, too infinite to hold, too eternal to touch, but only because it is right here and now, closer to you than your own breath, more inside you than your own thoughts, and closer to Spirit than all of them, this inside of You that is now reading this page, looking out at the world and wondering what it all means, when what-it-all-means is *you*. Not the you that can be seen, but the You that is doing the seeing.

The Seer in you, the Witness of this page and the entire world around it: it shimmers and scintillates with a thrilling bliss laced into the freedom of each and every moment, a searing soaring freedom that releases into infinity with every out-breath, tickling your spine with its radiant intensity as it razors from your body and into the great beyond, carrying gifts of infinite compassion and radical perfection and radiant care, gifts so outrageously huge your entire body would burst if it tried to contain them. You can feel it now, this Fullness that is yours pushing against you, trying to expand, this Freedom that is yours if you but stepped aside and

let it all come crashing through. And so it does, if you rest as the Witness of this and all the worlds that easily arise in your own awareness, worlds of your own making in each sunrise and each sunset, as the luminous orb transverses the vast sky of your own transparent emptiness. The great *radiant open* that is you, moment to moment, is *all* that ever is. Look! Look! Look! What do you see? What *can* you see? Except these textures of your own Self, this great One Taste of your own primordial Presence, everywhere appearing as the world. Is that world "out there" anything but the feeling of *you* right now? Listen to me:

Everything is you.
You are empty.
Empty is freely manifesting.
Freely manifesting is self liberating.

Join me, please, my friends, and let's do this one last time:

Notice your present awareness

Notice the objects arising in your awareness—the images and thoughts arising in your mind, the feelings and sensations arising in your body, the myriad objects arising around you in the room or environment. All of these are objects arising in your awareness.

Now think about what was in your awareness 5 minutes ago. Most of the thoughts have changed, most of the bodily sensations have changed, and probably most of the environment has changed. But something has not changed. Something in you is the same now as it was 5 minutes ago. What is present now that was present 5 minutes ago?

I AMness. The feeling-awareness of I AMness is still present. I am that ever-present I AMness. That I AMness is present now, it was present a moment ago, it was present a minute ago, it was present 5 minutes ago.

What was present 5 hours ago?

I AMness. That sense of I AMness is an ongoing, self-knowing, self-recognizing, self-validating I AMness. It is present now, it was present 5 hours ago. All my thoughts have changed, all my bodily sensations have changed, my environment has changed, but I AM is ever-present, radiant, open, empty, clear, spacious, transparent, free. Objects have changed, but not this formless I AMness. This obvious and present I AMness is present now as it was present 5 hours ago.

What was present 5 years ago?

I AMness. So many objects have come and gone, so many feelings have come and gone, so many thoughts have come and gone, so many dramas and terrors and loves and hates have come, and stayed awhile, and gone. But one thing has not come, and one thing has not gone. What is that? What is the only thing present in your awareness right now that you can remember was present 5 years ago? This timeless, ever-present feeling of I AMness is present now as it was 5 years ago.

What was present 5 centuries ago?

All that is ever-present is I AMness. Every person feels this same I AMness—because it is not a body, it is not a thought, it is not an object, it is not the environment, it is not anything that can be seen, but rather is the ever-present Seer, the ongoing open and empty Witness of all that is arising, in any person, in any world, in any place, at any time, in all the worlds until the end of time, there is only and always this obvious and immediate I AMness. What else could you possibly know? What else does anybody ever know? There is only and always this radiant, self-knowing, self-feeling, self-transcending I AMness, whether present now, 5 minutes ago, 5 hours ago, 5 centuries ago.

5 millennia ago?

Before Abraham was, I AM. Before the universe was, I AM. This is my original Face, the face I had before my parents were born, the face I had before the universe was born, the Face I had for all eternity until I decided to play this round of hide and seek, and get lost in the objects of my own creation.

I will NEVER again pretend that I do not know or feel my own I AMness.

And with that, the game is undone. A million thoughts have come and gone, a million feelings have come and gone, a million objects have come and gone. But one thing has not come, and one thing has not gone: the great Unborn and the great Undying, which never enters or leaves the stream of time, a pure Presence above time, floating in eternity. I am this great, obvious, self-knowing, self-validating, self-liberating I AMness.

Before Abraham was, I AM.

I AM is none other than Spirit in 1st-person, the ultimate, the sublime, the radiant all-creating Self of the entire Kosmos, present in me and you and him and her and them—as the I AMness that each and every one of us feels.

Because in all the known universes, the overall number of I AMs is but one.

Rest as I AMness always, the exact I AMness you feel right now, which is Unborn Spirit itself shining in and as you. Assume your personal identity as well—as this or that object, or this or that self, or this and that thing—resting always in the Ground of it All, as this great and completely obvious I AMness, and get up and go on about your day, in the universe I AM created.

Books by Ken Wilber

The Spectrum of Consciousness (1977). An introduction to the full-spectrum model, the first to show, in a systematic way, how the great psychological systems of the West can be integrated with the great contemplative traditions of the East.

No Boundary: Eastern and Western Approaches to Personal Growth (1979). A simple and popular guide to psychologies and therapies available from both Western and Eastern sources; designated by Wilber as reflecting the "Romantic" phase of his early work.

The Atman Project: A Transpersonal View of Human Development (1980). The first psychological system to suggest a way of uniting Eastern and Western, conventional and contemplative, orthodox and mystical approaches into a single, coherent framework.

Up from Eden: A Transpersonal View of Human Evolution (1981). Drawing on theorists from Joseph Campbell to Jean Gebser, Wilber outlines humankind's evolutionary journey—and "dialectic of process"—from its primal past to its integral future.

The Holographic Paradigm and Other Paradoxes: Exploring the Leading Edge of Science (1982). An anthology of contributions by prominent scientists and thinkers on the dialogue between science and religion.

A Sociable God: Toward a New Understanding of Religion (1983). A scholarly introduction to a system of reliable methods by which to adjudicate the legitimacy and authenticity of any religious movement.

Eye to Eye: The Quest for the New Paradigm (1983). An examination of three realms of knowledge: the empirical realm of the senses, the rational realm of the mind, and the contemplative realm of the spirit.

Quantum Questions: Mystical Writings of the World's Great Physicists (1984). An anthology of nontechnical excerpts selected from the work of great physicists, including Heisenberg, Schroedinger, Einstein, de Broglie, Jeans, Planck, Pauli, and Eddington.

Transformations of Consciousness: Conventional and Contemplative Perspectives on Development, by Ken Wilber, Jack Engler, and Daniel P. Brown (1986). Nine essays exploring the full-spectrum model of human growth and development, from prepersonal to personal to transpersonal.

Spiritual Choices: The Problem of Recognizing Authentic Paths to Inner Transformation, edited by Dick Anthony, Bruce Ecker, and Ken Wilber (1987). Psychologists and spiritual teachers contribute to this study of religious movements, aimed at answering the dilemma of how to distinguish spiritual tyranny from legitimate spiritual authority.

Grace and Grit: Spirituality and Healing in the Life and Death of Treya Killam Wilber (1991). The moving story of Ken's marriage to Treya and the five-year journey that took them through her illness, treatment, and eventual death from breast cancer.

Sex, Ecology, Spirituality: The Spirit of Evolution (1995). The first volume of the Kosmos Trilogy and the book that introduced the 4-quadrant model. This tour de force of scholarship and vision traces the course of evolution from matter to life to mind (and possible higher future levels), and describes the common patterns that evolution takes in all three domains.

A Brief History of Everything (1996). A short, highly readable version of *Sex, Ecology, Spirituality*, written in an accessible, conversational style, without all the technical arguments and endnotes; the place to begin if new to his work.

The Eye of Spirit: An Integral Vision for a World Gone Slightly Mad (1997). Essays explore the Integral Approach to such fields as psychology, spirituality, anthropology, cultural studies, art and literary theory, ecology, feminism, and planetary transformation.

The Marriage of Sense and Soul: Integrating Science and Religion (1998). After surveying the world's great wisdom traditions and extracting features they all share, Wilber offers compelling arguments that not only are these compatible with scientific truth, they also share a similar scientific method.

The Essential Ken Wilber: An Introductory Reader (1998). Brief passages from Wilber's most popular books, imparting the essence and flavor of his writings for newcomers to his work.

One Taste: The Journals of Ken Wilber (1999). A lively and entertaining glimpse into a year in the life of Ken Wilber.

The Collected Works of Ken Wilber, vols. 1–8 (1999–2000). An ongoing series.

Integral Psychology: Consciousness, Spirit, Psychology, Therapy (2000). A landmark study introducing the first truly integral psychology, this model includes waves of development, streams of development, states of consciousness, and the self, and follows the course of each from subconscious to self-conscious to super-conscious.

A Theory of Everything: An Integral Vision for Business, Politics, Science, and Spirituality (2001). A compact summary of the Integral Approach as a genuine "world philosophy," noteworthy because it includes many real-world applications in various fields. A popular choice for introductory reading.

Boomeritis: A Novel That Will Set You Free (2002). A combination of brilliant scholarship and wicked parody, the novel targets one of the most stubborn obstacles to realizing the integral vision: a disease of pluralism plus narcissism that Wilber calls "boomeritis."

The Simple Feeling of Being: Embracing Your True Nature (2004). A collection of inspirational, mystical, and instructional passages drawn from Wilber's publications, compiled and edited by some of his senior students.

Integral Spirituality: A Startling New Role for Religion in the Modern and Postmodern World (2006). A theory of spirituality that honors the truths of premodernity, modernity, and postmodernity—including the revolutions in science and culture—while incorporating the essential insights of the great religions. This is a truly revolutionary book, hailed by critics as fundamentally changing the nature and role of religion and spirituality.

Credits

Creative Director: **Marco Morelli**
Zoosphere Creative Consulting, LLC (www.zoosphere.com)

Graphic Designer: **Paul Salamone** (www.paulsalamone.com)

Typeface courtesy of **Mario Feliciano**
(www.felicianotypefoundry.com)

Featured Artists

Rommel DeLeon (www.c4chaos.com)
pp. 6, 22–23, 24–25, 108–9, 140 (middle),
208–9, 210–11, 212

Todd Guess (www.toddguess.com)
pp. 14, 64, 78, 83, 156, 226

Karl Eschenbach (www.karleschenbach.com)
pp. 130, 160–61, 162–63, 164

Nomali Perera
pp. 60–61

Kim Smith (www.kesmit.com)
p. 219

Other Contributing Artists

Chad Baker/Ryan McVay — pp. 12–13
David Brunner — p. 19
Marinko Tarlac — p. 29
Paul Salamone — pp. 35 (earth image courtesy of NASA), 40, 54, 123, 146, 191
Kevin Russ — p. 45
Edward Koren — p. 52 (© The New Yorker Collection 1995 Edward Koren from cartoonbank.com. All Rights Reserved.)
Mark Pruitt — pp. 62–63
Joseph Jean Rolland Dubé — p. 69 (top)
Maartje van Caspel — pp. 69 (middle), 93 (top right)
Klaas Lingbeek van Kranen — p. 69 (bottom)
Alex Bramwell — p. 74
Joel Morrison and Ken Wilber — pp. 90, 110
Antonis Papantoniou — pp. 93 (top left), 190
Lisa F. Young — p. 93 (bottom left)
Lloyd Paulson — p. 93 (bottom right)
Peter Chen — pp. 99 (top left)
Amanda Rohde — pp. 99 (top right), 200 (middle)
Lise Gagne — p. 99 (bottom left)
Eliza Snow — p. 99 (bottom right)
Jim Jurica — p. 101
Kateryna Govorushchenko — p. 103
Ben Wright and Ken Wilber — pp. 119, 216
Elena Ray — pp. 126, 140 (top)
Vladimir Pomortsev — p. 140 (bottom)
Brand X Pictures — chap. 6, all "topographic body" images
Steve Self — p. 186
Andy Lim — p. 200 (left)
Oleg Prikhodko — p. 200 (right)

SUPPOSE WE TOOK EVERYTHING that all the various world cultures have to tell us about human potential—about psychological, spiritual, and social growth—and identified the basic patterns that connect these pieces of knowledge. What if we attempted to create an all-inclusive map that touches the most important factors from all of the world's great traditions?

Ken Wilber's Integral Vision provides just such a map. Using all the known systems and models of human growth—from the ancient sages to the latest breakthroughs in cognitive science—it distills their major components into five simple elements, and, moreover, ones that readers can verify in their own experience right now.

In any field of interest—such as business, law, science, psychology, health, art, or everyday living and learning—the Integral Vision ensures that we are utilizing the full range of resources for the situation, leading to a greater likelihood of success and fulfillment. With easily understood explanations, exercises, and familiar examples, *The Integral Vision* shows how we can accelerate growth and development to higher, wider, deeper ways of being, embodied in self, shared in community, and connected to the planet, which can literally help with everything from spiritual enlightenment to business success to personal relationships.

Ken Wilber is the author of over twenty books. He is the founder of Integral Institute, a think-tank for studying integral theory and practice, with outreach through local and online communities such as Integral Naked, Integral Education Network, Integral Training, and Integral Spiritual Center.

Cover design by Paul Salamone

©2007 Shambhala Publications, Inc.

Printed in China

www.shambhala.com

Shambhala
Boston & London

ISBN 978-1-59030-475-4

51895

9 781590 304754

US $18.95

CAN $22.50